# FREE FROM YOUR PAST

LEARNING TO LIVE
THE LIFE YOU'VE
ALWAYS WANTED

# ED TAYLOR

# Free from Your Past

learning to live the life you've always wanted

**Ed Taylor**

ABOUNDING GRACE
MEDIA GROUP™

# Dedication

*My life's ministry and this book are dedicated to Jesus Christ.*

*I'm especially grateful for my wife Marie and kids, Joshua and Caitlin, with deep memories of our son Eddie and his son, our grandson Levi (#onedaylittleguy).*

*This book is for all those crippled by their past, tainted by sin, but hopeful for change. God is ready to work deeply in your heart, mind, and soul! Trust Him.*

*Thank you Catherine McDaugale for the investment of time in helping me edit these Bible studies into a readable book format.*

*Thank you Marie and Julie for your proofreading and suggestions.*

*Thank you Pastors Skip Heitzig, Chuck Smith, Jeff Johnson, Greg Laurie, Warren Wiersbe, and so many others who have taught and mentored me through your ministries.*

*And a HUGE THANK YOU to the fellowship family of Calvary Church, whose love and support mean so much to us.*

*There is therefore now no condemnation to those who are in Christ Jesus, who do not walk according to the flesh, but according to the Spirit.*

— Romans 8:1

# Contents

# Introduction

Are you being taunted by your past? Do you feel condemned by the things you've done or by what has happened to you? If so, this is something you really need to hear. The Bible teaches us,

> There is therefore now *no condemnation to those who are in Christ Jesus*, who do not walk according to the flesh, but according to the Spirit. (Romans 8:1 (emphasis added))

Did you catch that? You're not condemned if you're in Christ. In Christ is a great place to be.

- In Christ, your sin has been judged. The penalty has been paid in Jesus.
- In Christ, your sins have been forgiven and washed away. Your sins have been blotted out like a thick cloud (Isaiah 44:22). Blotted out, gone.
- In Christ, God hasn't dealt with you according to your iniquities. He has removed your sins as far as the east is from the west (Psalm 103:10, 12).
- In Christ, your sins have been cast into the depths of the sea (Micah 7:19).

## Introduction

It's great to be in Christ.

But there's still a problem in your life. You have a past. It's like a shadow, a cloud that follows you around. You can tell yourself there's no condemnation because you're in Christ. But what should you do with your past now that you know that truth?

We all have a past—pasts that mock and plague us. Ones that shoot arrows of condemnation at us. Our pasts try to undermine our faith. And our pasts follow us around wherever we go.

For example, it doesn't matter where you go today. Wherever you are, '80s music is playing. It's everywhere. You can't turn it off.

While '80s music may mean nothing to you, do you know what '80s music does to me? It takes me back to the '80s. Do you want to know when I did the most damage to my life and to other people's lives? The '80s.

There are certain episodes in my life that are actually tied to a song. When a song comes on the radio, it takes me right back to that day. I may not have thought about it in 15 years. But when I hear that song, I'm right back there.

And that's happened quite a few times. I needed to make a decision in my life that I'm not in the '80s anymore. Isn't that great? I don't live in the '80s. It's true. Today's the day of salvation. Today's the day that Jesus has redeemed me and changed me.

So, I don't care if I hear those goofy songs. I'm not in the '80s anymore. God has changed my life. The Ed of the '80s is dead.

It's the same in your life. There are all sorts of things trying to drag you back to the past. Thoughts. Memories. Pictures. The enemy has your number. He knows that you've tied a situation in your life to a specific song or a specific scent or a specific place. He knows that.

It's constantly before you because the enemy knows that, if he can get you to look backward, you'll be stuck. And if you're stuck, you're not going anywhere. You're only going down. And so, he wants to pull you back.

Now, your past might not be as bad as mine. My past might not be as bad as yours. But we all have a past. And you likely have something in your life that you would wipe away if you had the chance. If you could, you would permanently erase it. For many, it's a constant shadow in your life.

I know I'm not proud of my past. There's a lot I wish I had avoided. I don't like it. You know that philosophical question: If you could do anything to change your past, would you do it? Of course, I would want to avoid a lot of my sinful pain. I wouldn't want to hurt people like I did.

But at the same time, I'm who I am today as a culmination of my past. So, if it meant changing my past and not being where I am today, then the answer is no. It's a trick question. The answer really is to accept my life as from the Lord.

Sure, I wish a big section of it wasn't there. But my past is a testimony that God has done a work. There's no question that God has done a work in my life.

I don't know what's in your past. Some of you had a very difficult past and made some really bad choices. Others took a moral path and chose to do the right thing even before they came to Christ.

Whatever is in your past, we're all touched by sin. We all have difficulties. Whether you grew up in a hopeless situation or were raised in a godly home, the enemy will use your past against you. The enemy will bring up the way your dad treated you, the way your mom spoke to you, or the way you treated people. Your past has a way of following you.

I remember the first time my past was used against me. I had a criminal record from mistakes I had made under the influence. I applied for a job, and they ran a background check. I told the man that I was a born-again Christian and didn't live that way anymore. But he said, "Well, we don't hire thieves here." And that was it. He didn't even give me a chance.

It was devastating. It was a reminder that, although God is quick to forgive us and forget our sins, our world is not so quick to forgive or forget. And we're not always so quick to forgive ourselves.

As your past follows you, you need to learn how to navigate your world as a believer in Jesus Christ, even if it's just in your own mind. You can enjoy freedom from the past that follows you, taunts you, and even condemns you.

Although you can't change your past, you can hold on to the glorious truth in Romans 8:1. The word *now* in that verse is so important. There is therefore *now*—every time you read it, every time you meditate on it, every time you think about it—no condemnation. Now. *In . . . this . . . moment.* Every second of every minute.

There is no condemnation for your past, every time you say that verse. There is *now* no condemnation to those who are in Christ Jesus, who do not walk according to the flesh, but according to the Spirit.

If you look in the New King James Version, you'll notice a little asterisk in that verse. The asterisk means that the last part of that verse—*who do not walk according to the flesh, but according to the Spirit*—is in some, but not all, of the earliest manuscripts that we have. Either way, it's a very powerful truth that is repeated in Romans 8:4.

You can only fully experience this truth when you're walking in the Spirit. Although you're not condemned as a born-again believer when you're *not* walking in the Spirit, there are consequences. When you're in the flesh—caught up in yourself and not in the Spirit—you beat yourself up. You heap loads of condemnation on yourself. We don't need someone else to do it for us. We're often our own worst critics.

Even when we walk in the Spirit, there's always the enemy of our souls accusing us and trying to condemn us. But, in Christ, there's freedom and safety.

So, living with the reality of a past, the question remains: What do you do with your past?

The good news is that, if you're in Christ—if you're a born-again believer—you don't have to stay in your past. Because there's no condemnation from God, you don't have to be stuck there. You don't have to be trapped or paralyzed by it. You don't have to relive it in your mind over and over again. You don't have to be defined by it.

In Christ, you can move forward. You can live in the present. Jesus has already set you free from your past. You just need to walk in that freedom.

This book will show you how to walk in the freedom that comes from being in Christ. You'll learn how to deal with your past and the anger that consumes you because of the things you've gone through or the things you've done. It's possible to walk in freedom, living moment by moment in Jesus.

# CHAPTER ONE

## Dealing With Condemnation

Condemnation is a heavy and burdensome word. The word condemn means "to declare to be reprehensible, wrong, or evil"; "to pronounce guilty"; to sentence someone; to "doom" someone.[1]

Houses are condemned. And when a house is condemned, it's torn down and never used again. Not only are houses condemned, but criminals are condemned. Some spend many years in prison. Others never leave prison. It's a heavy word.

So, have you ever felt condemned? Have you ever felt like a decision was made against you? Or has someone declared you to be guilty?

Maybe you were driving down the road, minding your own business, when you saw flashing lights behind you in your rearview mirror. You were hoping they were for someone else, but they were for you. You looked at the lights. And then, where did your eyes go next? Right to the speedometer.

It's a natural response. Your eyes go to the speedometer, and your foot comes off the accelerator. Even if you put your foot on the brakes, it's too late. You're already busted. It makes you feel like you did as a kid in the principal's office.

So, you pull over. You put your hands on the steering wheel and roll the window down. And the police officer comes up and says, "How are you? Can I see your driver's license and registration?" As the officer walks away, you wait. You begin to calculate what it'll mean for the cost of your insurance and how hard it's going to be to write that check.

The officer finally comes back after running everything and says, "Sir, I'm just going to give you a warning this time. But you know this area has a lot of kids playing in it, and you need to slow down."

And then everything changes. You begin to worship the Lord, "Hallelujah! Thank you, Jesus. What a relief." Now you're going to use cruise control all the way home. You are never going to speed again for the rest of your life.

You know that feeling of relief. Now multiply that by ten billion. Because that's what God's grace has done for us in the spiritual realm. You know you've done wrong. And you know you've made mistakes. You know what you deserve. Yet, because of God's grace, you don't get what you deserve. As Paul wrote to the Romans,

> There is therefore now no condemnation to those who are in Christ Jesus, who do not walk according to the flesh, but according to the Spirit. (Romans 8:1)

In Christ, there is no condemnation. If you look up the word *no* in Greek, it means no. But let me give you a deeper sense of this word. The word *no* here means, no possibility for condemnation. None. Zip. Zero. Nada.

I know the spiritual battle gets heavy sometimes. It's not easy. You get tired of fighting. You no longer want to be in the battle of the flesh against the Spirit.

And we don't always win the battles. There isn't always success. It's easy to get caught up in your feelings. And when you're in the realm of feelings, it begins to feel like you'll never make it. It's too much. When you fail—and failure will come to all of us—there's a sense of guilt and shame that can easily lead to self-condemnation.

But for those who are in Christ Jesus, there is no condemnation. Your past sins are forgiven. Your present sins are forgiven. And your future sins are forgiven.

Salvation in Jesus Christ is the whole package. You're not saved one piece at a time. When a man or a woman is born again, God saves you as a whole package. Your salvation is complete.

God doesn't work in time like we do. We live on a linear plane where there is yesterday, today, and tomorrow. But God is outside of time. He lives in the eternal now. And God saves you while knowing everything about you—everything you've ever done and everything you'll ever do.

## *Are You Prone to Condemnation?*

Too many Christians—maybe even you—live under a sense of condemnation. They think they've done something wrong and God cannot forgive them. Some even go further to say God *won't* forgive them.

If you're prone to self-condemnation, here are six things to look out for in your life.

1 **You always feel guilty.**
In your mind, you lean on the side of guilt. Even when you haven't done anything wrong, you feel guilty. Your guilty conscience never seems to go away.

. . .

## 2 You're often motivated by guilt.

When someone lays a guilt trip on you, you spring into action. It moves you. And even if someone doesn't, you do it on your own. You interpret things from a guilty perspective.

## 3 You're a people pleaser.

You're continually looking for people to accept, appreciate, notice, and applaud you. When you do good, you expect people to tell you. When you don't get that validation from others, you feel bad about yourself. And that feeling is one step away from condemning yourself.

## 4 You feel like God is mad at you.

Your mistakes are always plaguing you. When you sit down to read your Bible, you feel like God is mad at you. And when you start to pray, you feel like God is mad at you. You truly have a sense that God is displeased with you. You may acknowledge that God is not mad at others, but you think He's always angry with you.

## 5 You never feel like you do enough.

You could serve in your church for hundreds of hours or pray all night long, but you still wonder if you should have done more. Let's say you make a commitment to go on a five-hour prayer walk. After five hours of walking and praying, instead of being encouraged, you think, *Ah, I could have done six hours.* And you beat yourself up because you always feel like you could have or should have done more.

. . .

6 **You always live in the past.**
You live in the past—not the good past but the bad past. The things that you've done are always on your mind, even if you did them 25 years ago. You can't stop thinking about them even if they've been long since resolved. You're enslaved by your past.

If you have a tendency toward self-condemnation, what do you do? Start by accepting the fact that if you've asked for forgiveness for your sins—the mistakes you've made—God has forgiven you. The forgiveness of God comes with repentance. And if you are in Christ, there's no condemnation.

## How to Know If You're in Christ

So, since there's no condemnation for those who are in Christ, the real question is: Are you in Christ?

The question is not as hard as it sounds. Let me ask you a different question that you can answer right away. Are you reading this book in your house? That's not a hard question to answer. Because you know where you are. Either you're in your house, or you're not.

The same holds true for the question of whether you're in Christ. You're either in Christ, or you're not. You're either born again into the body of Christ, or you're not.

You may be thinking, *I don't know if I'm in Christ because I blew it this week.* Or maybe you wonder, *I don't know because I've got these thoughts.* The mistakes you've made and the thoughts you've had don't affect your position in Christ. You're either born again, or you're not. You're either in Christ, or you're not.

I'm not asking if you were raised in a religious home or if you were baptized as an infant. You're not in Christ simply by going to church on a Sunday morning or because you attended one all of your life. The question is not whether your grandmother was religious or if you've said a prayer here or there. I'm not asking if you're better than the worst person you can think of.

The question is: Have you been born again? You can know you've been born again if you've repented of your sins and acknowledged God as your Creator and His Son Jesus Christ as your Savior—if you've surrendered your life to Him.

Being a born-again believer is a place of surrender. You're no longer living your way. Instead, you want to do things God's way. You won't do things perfectly. You'll still make mistakes. But you surrender your life to God.

It's the same as when you're in your house. When you're at home, you're not somewhere else. You're at home.

When you're in Christ Jesus, you're in Him every moment of your life. If you've truly asked Jesus to come into your life and forgive you of your sins—if you've confessed with your mouth the Lord Jesus and believe in your heart that God has raised Him from the dead (Romans 10:9)—you can say that you're in Christ.

### The Benefits of Being in Christ

Although the Old Covenant was based on what you needed to do to be right with God, the New Covenant rests on better promises. God has given us many promises about who we are in Christ. The benefits of being in Christ are overwhelming. There are at least 90 statements in the Bible about who you are in Christ. Here are just a few of them:

- In Christ, you've been justified freely (Romans 3:24).
- In Christ, you're now dead to sin (Romans 6:11). It doesn't have the same power over you anymore. This is a very powerful truth. God has given you power, residing inside of you, to live apart from sin. Before you were born again, all you did was sin. You were

dead in your trespasses and sin. But now, in Christ, you are dead *to* sin and no longer dead *in* sin.

- In Christ, you have eternal life and the hope of heaven (Romans 6:23).
- In Christ, you will never be separated from the love of God (Romans 8:39).
- In Christ, you're part of a new family (Romans 12:5). You've been adopted into a body of believers. It doesn't matter what separates us on the outward— your nationality or the color of your skin. In Christ, we're one, big family. It doesn't matter where you go in the world or what language you speak. When you find a believer, you've got family, because we have Jesus in common.
- In Christ, you have hope (Romans 15:8). Your hope is in Jesus, not in this world. Your hope is in Christ, not in government, politics, a president, or a mayor. Your hope is not in man. The Bible actually warns us not to put our trust in man (Psalm 146:3–4).
- In Christ, you have reason to glory, a reason to live (Romans 15:17). You have a purpose to serve and live your life to the fullest.
- In Christ, you're sanctified (1 Corinthians 1:2). That means you've been set apart to be changed. Every single day you live, God is changing you and conforming you into the image of Jesus Christ. Even your worst days are used by God.
- In Christ, God is working all things together for good (Romans 8:28). All of it. Nothing's wasted.
- In Christ, you're a new person—old things have passed away and all things have become new (2 Corinthians 5:17).

A full list of God's promises about who you are in Christ is in

Chapter 7. All of those truths are yours to hold on to. Take time to go through each one. You'll be encouraged as you do. The moment you were born again, you received all of Jesus Christ into your life. And every day since then, you're becoming conformed a little bit more into His image.

## The Danger of NOT Being in Christ

But for those who aren't in Christ—for those who aren't born again—the Bible paints a stark contrast. It's as clear as black and white. If you don't have Jesus, your life is in spiritual peril. And it's not getting better. Your life is filled with confusion, guilt, bondage, neglect, and condemnation.

It's why we're seeing the number of suicides rise to epic proportions. People are hopeless. There's nowhere to turn in this world that will give you the satisfaction that comes from Jesus.

We're living in a society that's calling good, evil and evil, good. Our legislators are making decisions that are hurting society and making things worse. Legalizing drugs, like marijuana, won't solve any problems. One of the worst things you can do is to take away the sensitivity and clarity of someone's mind. Marijuana is a gateway drug. It's not the end. It's the beginning of something really, really bad. Making it legal doesn't stop it from hurting people.

You see, when you're not in Christ, you make really bad decisions. And then you heap loads of condemnation on yourself.

By the time someone shared the gospel with me, they didn't need to explain the issue of my sin. They didn't have to give me a list of a hundred sins from the Bible and hope that one of them would hit my soul.

While I didn't use the word sin, I knew about my bad behavior. I was well aware of those times when I woke up face down somewhere in the city after the alcohol wore off because, the night before, I had done something so bad that my friends had pulled the car over, opened the door, and kicked me out.

Apart from Christ, I couldn't get away from my worry and anxiety. I was always waking up with myself. After a night of drinking myself into darkness, I would wake up and wonder what I had done. Then when I found out, I would think, *I just can't believe it. What kind of person am I?*

And then, at a young age in jail, I told myself, *I'm done. It's over. I've thrown my life away. It's going to end a lot earlier than I ever expected, so I might as well go out strong.* Even though I was surrounded by people who loved me—even with a son and a wife—it didn't matter. Why? Because I wasn't in Christ. I was in Ed. And being in Ed is a bad place to be.

You don't want to be in this world, living for this world, and thinking that this is where your source of satisfaction will be. It will only bring condemnation. That's why, when you're in the flesh, condemnation messes with your head. Because you've lost the sense of being in Christ.

Being in the flesh doesn't change your status as a believer. But it pulls you closer to the life you lived before you were saved. *In Christ is the place of safety. You're secure in Him.* On top of that, you have the indwelling of the Holy Spirit in your life, not letting you get away with anything. The Holy Spirit draws you and convicts you to bring you back to Christ. In Christ is the place of safety. You're secure in Him. It's a place of strength.

As Jesus put it, "And this is the condemnation, that the light has come into the world, and men loved darkness rather than light, because their deeds were evil" (John 3:19). That's the condemnation. Condemnation is not in Christ. It's apart from Christ.

And if you're reading this and you haven't been born again, today is the day. Now is the time. I don't know where you think your life is going to end. But the Bible says, apart from Christ, your life is going to end eternally separated from God. And that will be your just reward.

Make no mistake about it—God is fair, and God is just. And He's the One who sacrificed His own Son to pay the penalty of your sin. A sinless God meets you in your helpless state. Why? Because He loves you. And He's patient with you, so He might rescue you from yourself.

### The Importance of Remembering This Truth

But for those who are born again, condemnation can enter our lives because we forget. We forget the bondage that sin holds. It can be easy to walk away from God's faithfulness even if it's just in our minds.

In John 8, we meet a woman who was caught in the very act of her sin. In the very act—a very humiliating place to be.

The act? Well, it was a sexual act. The Bible speaks of it as adultery, which means she was having sex with a man who was not her husband. And by the time they dragged her into Jesus' presence, the act of adultery was in her past. Although she was caught *in* the act, it took some time to get her from the act to Jesus.

By the way, the woman was set up. She was used as a pawn. That's what religion does. It uses people. The religious rulers set her up. Even if they did so because that sin was part of her background, it doesn't matter. She was used, and that's always a sin.

Anyway, by the time they got her into the presence of Jesus, the act was in the past. She's no longer engaged in that sinful act. So, let's look at what happens.

Now early in the morning He [Jesus] came again into the temple, and all the people came to Him; and He sat down and taught them. Then the scribes and Pharisees brought to Him a woman caught in adultery. And when they had set her in the midst, they said to Him, "Teacher, this woman was caught in adultery, in the very act." (John 8:2–4)

We read that in a clean, sterile environment. But it was not clean or sterile. It was messy. It was tumultuous, probably loud. She's disheveled. It doesn't even speak of her being covered up. But I hope she was.

And they brought her to Jesus, tears streaming. Their faces were fixed with anger. Not at her, she's just a pawn. They're abusing her. They wanted Jesus. They wanted to take Him out. So, they brought this defenseless woman whom they had set up.

Let me remind you that abuse in any form in Jesus' Church is a sin. It is not from God. It's not God's will for any pastor, any lay leader, or anyone in His Church to perpetrate abuse of any kind on you, male or female, especially in the name of God.

And then the scribes and Pharisees told Jesus, "Now Moses, in the law, commanded us that such should be stoned" (John 8:5). If they really believed what Moses said, they would have done it already. But they didn't because then they asked Jesus,

"But what do You say?" This they said, testing Him, that they might have something of which to accuse Him. But Jesus stooped down and wrote on the ground with His finger, as though He did not hear.

So when they continued asking Him, He raised Himself up and said to them, "He who is without sin among you, let him throw a stone at her first." And again He stooped down and wrote on the ground. Then those who heard it, being convicted by their conscience, went out one by one, beginning with the oldest even to the last. And Jesus was left alone, and the woman standing in the midst. (John 8:5–9)

You see, they had past sin too. And they're living in the present sin. We've all sinned and fallen short of the glory of God (Romans 3:23). As Jesus was writing on the ground, they still weren't repentant. The religious rulers still weren't changing. The woman wasn't getting any attention now. Jesus was dealing with them.

Then notice in verse 10—Jesus said to her,

"Woman, where are those accusers of yours? Has no one condemned you?"

She said, "No one, Lord."

And Jesus said to her, "Neither do I condemn you; go and sin no more." (John 8:10–11)

Pay attention to those words. If you battle condemnation, receive them, no matter the sin. *Neither do I condemn you.* Circle, underline, or highlight them in your Bible. *Neither do I condemn you; go and sin no more.* That's all that she needed.

I don't know why, but sometimes I argue with God. I can hear the voice of Jesus saying to me, "Neither do I condemn you, Ed; go and sin no more." And yet, I condemn myself or allow others to condemn me.

Perhaps some of you have found yourself in that same place. Jesus says, "Neither do I condemn you; go and sin no more. I forgive you. Past, present, and future, I forgive you." In Christ, you're forgiven. And God's promise of forgiveness is all throughout the Bible.

- Through Isaiah, God said, "I have blotted out, like a thick cloud, your transgressions, and like a cloud, your sins. Return to Me, for I have redeemed you" (Isaiah 44:22).
- David said, "He has not dealt with us according to our sins, nor punished us according to our iniquities. For

as the heavens are high above the earth, so great is His mercy toward us who fear Him" (Psalm 103:10–11).

- God also spoke through Isaiah to tell us, "I, even I, am He who blots out your transgressions for My own sake; and I will not remember your sins" (Isaiah 43:25).
- Peter said, "Repent therefore and be converted, that your sins may be blotted out, so that times of refreshing may come from the presence of the Lord" (Acts 3:19).
- And Paul said, "There is therefore now no condemnation to those who are in Christ" (Romans 8:1).

So, answer this question for me: Are you in Christ? It's that simple. In Christ, there's no condemnation.

## Living in Christ Apart from Condemnation

As you move forward in your life in Christ, remember that you are no longer condemned by your past. You have the freedom to move away from your past and into your future. Here are a few practical tips to help you live your life in Christ apart from condemnation.

1 **Don't confuse condemnation with conviction.**
Condemnation and conviction are two very different things. Conviction of sin is a good thing. It's from God, and we need it. It's wholesome and valuable. The conviction of the Holy Spirit brings life and correction. On the other hand, condemnation brings death.

A simple way to remember it is this: the conviction of sin draws you *to* God but condemnation leads you *away* from God.

For example, people often avoid going to church when they're under the weight of condemnation. When you're under the weight of condemnation, church is not an attractive place to be. You misunderstand everything that God says. You interpret it through glasses of condemnation. And when you put on the glasses of condemnation, even the best encouragement is misinterpreted.

*Remember that the Holy Spirit will never condemn you. Never.*

God wants to free you from sin. When Jesus ministered to this precious woman, He told her it was sin. He said, "Don't do it. Leave it behind you. Don't get caught up in this anymore. This life isn't good for you." When everybody left and it was just Jesus and this woman under the weight of condemnation, He asked her, "Has no one condemned you? Well, I'm not condemning you either. But go and sin no more."

Remember that the Holy Spirit will never condemn you. Never. The enemy of our soul—he's the accuser of the brethren (Revelation 12:10).

## 2 When you're convicted of sin, repent.

You can say you're sorry and never really mean it. True repentance will lead you away from the sin. That's what repentance means.

The first step towards repentance is confession. That means you see your sin like God does. The Bible says, "If we confess our sins, He is faithful and just to forgive us our sins and to cleanse us from all unrighteousness" (1 John 1:9).

Confession and repentance; if you're struggling in this area, read Psalm 51. It's often referred to as the psalm of repentance. It was written by David who had much to repent from. David not only committed adultery; he had the woman's husband killed.

Let the Holy Spirit use that psalm to do a work in your life. God will empower you, strengthen you, and help you.

## 3 Believe and act on God's Word.

I know it sounds simple. But when you hear something, do it. For example, you've learned in this chapter the life-giving message of Romans 8:1—there is therefore now no condemnation for those who are in Christ. Believe what God said in that verse. Take the promise. Trust that God meant what He said—there's no condemnation for you in Christ.

You know where you're at right now. You might be arguing with me, saying, "But Ed . . . ." But it's not about me. *God* said there's no condemnation for you. So it's not about me or even about you. It's about Him. It's about the freedom He wants to give you.

Jesus looks at you and says, "Well, has anyone condemned you?" Unfortunately, you can't necessarily answer that question, "No," like the woman did.

But even if there are people condemning you right now, remember that it's not from God. Jesus would still say to you, "I'm not condemning you. Go and sin no more."

The simplicity of the Bible is life-giving. The Bible is alive and powerful. It's sharper than any two-edged sword (Hebrews 4:12). So, it makes sense that the enemy tries to keep you from it. It makes sense that, when you're in your flesh, you try to avoid it.

Have you ever noticed that distractions arise when you try to read the Bible? If you use your phone to read it, because that's convenient for you, a text message pops up. You answer the text message, and it takes you to Instagram. Before you know it, you've got to go to work. You tell yourself, *Well, I'll read it when I take a break.* But then you've got a phone call during your break.

And then it's lunchtime, but you can't find your phone. The distractions can be endless.

It makes sense. The enemy wants to separate you from the life-giving words of the Scriptures. Because if you don't hear the Word, you won't know the Word. And if you don't know the Word, you won't act on the Word.

Yet, God has made things so easy for us. He doesn't require you to be a scholar, have a degree, or go to seminary. Just read the Bible. God doesn't even say you have to understand it. Just read it and do it.

If you don't understand something, it will drive you to God to ask Him what it means. So, you're going to win either way. And if you don't know what a word means, look it up. There are a lot of resources where you can look up words. Don't make excuses.

As you learn what God's Word says, believe it and do it. Take the access God has given you. As the Bible says in Romans 5,

> Therefore, having been justified by faith, we have peace with God through our Lord Jesus Christ, through whom also we have access by faith into this grace in which we stand, and rejoice in hope of the glory of God. (Romans 5:1–2)

We have access by faith. Obey that word. Come in and take the access.

If you have doubts that you are saved, believe what Jesus told us in John 5. He said, "Most assuredly, I say to you, he who hears My word and believes in Him who sent Me has everlasting life" (John 5:24).

If you hear Jesus' Word and believe in the One who sent Him, you have everlasting life. You're saved. Don't give in to the doubt. Believe God's Word. God says "if you confess with your mouth the Lord Jesus and believe in your heart that God has raised Him from the dead, you will be saved" (Romans 10:9). So, live as a saved person.

We live by what God has said in the Bible because His Word is life. We don't live by our feelings. We don't live by our experiences.

It makes me think of Noah. Noah is a great example in the Hall of Faith in Hebrews 11:7. Noah built an ark out of obedience, not understanding. Noah had no idea

*We live by what God has said in the Bible because His Word is life.*

what a flood was, let alone a drop of rain. He just heard God's Word, and he did it. And they mocked him. They made fun of him.

Who knows how Noah felt and what he thought? I wonder if he felt silly, building a big boat when the world had never seen a drop of rain. I wonder if his wife pointed her finger at him and said, "You're crazy. Get that thing out of the front yard."

But he obeyed. Noah didn't build the ark because he felt like it. He built it because God commanded him.

Noah gives us an example to follow. He heard. He believed. And he acted. Doing those things will change your life.

4 **Stop looking back.**
No more looking back. Receive the word from Romans 8:1. There is therefore now no condemnation to those who are in Christ. Memorize it. Believe it. Live it. A life of abiding in Christ does not lead to condemnation. It leads to victory and freedom and a remembrance of all that God has done on your behalf.

# CHAPTER TWO

## Dealing With The Law Of God

In Romans 7, we read the confessions of an exhausted believer. Looking back on his life, the apostle Paul relived his own past—the wrestling and the struggles he went through. He wrote about how the law bound him tightly with all of its rules and regulations. Paul had been bound and married to the law. The law was perfect, and it seemed to have no escape.

But there was an escape. The escape was not physical; it was spiritual death. When, by faith, he married Jesus Christ—the One who fulfilled the law—he was released from the expectations, demands, and perfections of the law.

You too are released from the law when you place your faith in Jesus Christ, die to yourself, and live unto Christ. The way to be free from the demands of the law is to live as a new creation in Christ. In Christ, you are a new creation, "old things have passed away; behold, all things have become new" (2 Corinthians 5:17).

## The Battle between the Spirit and the Flesh

Yet, in the freedom from the law and in the newness of life in Jesus, there's still a problem. All of us who live by faith in Jesus still have our flesh—the carnality of our minds; the legality of our humanity.

When the word flesh is used spiritually in the Bible, it's not a reference to the skin on your bones. It's not a physical statement. Instead, it means to live according to your own resources. It's literally the opposite of Proverbs 3:5, which tells us to "[t]rust in the Lord with all your heart, and lean not on your own understanding."

*What man is unable to do after years of trying, God is able to do in a millisecond of time . . .*

When you lean on your own understanding, you're in the flesh. You're relying on your own resources. As smart as you may be and as smart as you might become, you will never be as smart as God. And your resources and abilities pale in comparison to God's power. What man is unable to do after years of trying, God is able to do in a millisecond of time, by the presence of the Holy Spirit.

There is a battle between the flesh and the Spirit. Everything is tainted by sin. Even on our best days, we're imperfect. The best that we can offer God is imperfect and tainted by sin.

So, when you hear the phrase *battling the flesh*, think of it as a battle against your old sinful habit patterns. Let's say you're in the garage, hammering a nail into a piece of wood and you hit your thumb really hard. Your first response will give you a good idea of your flesh. You'll likely blurt out something that you haven't heard come out of your mouth in 20 years. Why? Because you're in the flesh, and it was a bad habit to say those words in your past. Those patterns still exist in your life.

The same holds true even if it doesn't come out of your

mouth. Maybe instead, you just thought it in your head. But the words still came up, even if you didn't say them.

When the Bible says that you're a new creation in Christ, it speaks of your spiritual life that's being renewed day by day. But your brain is still the same old brain in your head. God is renewing your mind. You're growing in grace. Yet, you still have a battle with your flesh.

For those of us who got saved later in life, we have deeper-set sinful habits. We may not be living in those sinful habits anymore. Praise God for that! That should no longer be the manner of your life. But because it was part of your past, it becomes a point of battle against your flesh. As the Bible tells us, "For the flesh lusts against the Spirit, and the Spirit against the flesh; and these are contrary to one another, so that you do not do the things that you wish" (Galatians 5:17).

The word lust means a strong craving. We almost always use the word lust when we're talking about sexual sin. In that context, it means you have a strong craving for sexual sin. But the word can actually be used to describe a strong craving for a lot of things.

So, when the Bible says the Spirit lusts against the flesh, it means there's a battle over what you will yield to in your life. Will you yield to the indwelling power of God in you—the Holy Spirit—who longs to please God and wants to lead you in the paths of righteousness and purity? Or will you yield to your own sinful habits?

There was a season in Paul's life when he went back under the law, underneath its rules and regulations. Rules and regulations can feel like a place of safety. For instance, you might decide,

*I've had a bad day. So, starting tomorrow, I'm going to get up at 7:00 a.m., open my Bible, journal, and do my devos for exactly 15 minutes. Then on Friday, I'll do them for*

*20 minutes. And on Saturday, for 25 minutes. On Sunday,
I'm going to get up extra early. Not only am I going to do my
devos, I'm going to go to church on top of that. And I might
even stay after.*

Then you start setting it up. Your rules are meaningful.
They're attainable. And when you do them, you feel good.

So, what do you do? You wake up at 7:00 a.m. the next day, do
your devos, and think, *Ah, that felt good. I'm so right with God.*

But then you have a bad day. You don't get up at 7:00 a.m. By
setting up a law for yourself and failing to keep it, the law
condemns you and accuses you. And it uses your voice to do it.
*You didn't get up at 7:00 a.m.* And you answer; *I know, I'm a
horrible Christian.*

And then you make a mistake in the afternoon. You get mad
at your kids. And you think, *I'm a horrible mom.*

Or you mess up at work and tell yourself, *I'm a horrible
employee.*

Why? Because you didn't keep your own rules. You set up a
system that took you away from the grace of God—away from
enjoying Him—through the good and the bad. And I hope you
know that even if you woke up at 7:05 a.m. and forgot your
devos, God still loves you. He still cares for you.

That's what Paul was wrestling with in Romans 7. He gave us
insight into what it feels like. This might be in your life. He said,

For we know that the law is spiritual, but I am carnal, sold
under sin. For what I am doing, I do not understand. For what I
will to do, that I do not practice; but what I hate, that I do. If,
then, I do what I will not to do, I agree with the law that it is
good. But now, it is no longer I who do it, but sin that dwells in
me. For I know that in me (that is, in my flesh) nothing good
dwells. (Romans 7:14–18)

Nothing good dwells in us. The good in your life comes from your relationship with Jesus Christ. And He's making you better every day. Jesus is developing you and pouring more of Himself into you as you yield your life to Him.

## *The Law Cannot Change You*

Paul knew that nothing good dwelt in him. He recognized that he couldn't change himself. And he knew that the law couldn't change him either. Paul continued,

> for to will is present with me, but how to perform what is good I do not find. For the good that I will to do, I do not do; but the evil I will not to do, that I practice. Now if I do what I will not to do, it is no longer I who do it, but sin that dwells in me.
>
> I find then a law, that evil is present with me, the one who wills to do good. For I delight in the law of God according to the inward man. But I see another law in my members, warring against the law of my mind, and bringing me into captivity to the law of sin which is in my members. O wretched man that I am! Who will deliver me from this body of death? I thank God —through Jesus Christ our Lord!
>
> So then, with the mind I myself serve the law of God, but with the flesh the law of sin.
>
> There is therefore now no condemnation to those who are in Christ Jesus, who do not walk according to the flesh, but according to the Spirit. For the law of the Spirit of life in Christ Jesus has made me free from the law of sin and death. For what the law could not do in that it was weak through the flesh, God did by sending His own Son in the likeness of sinful flesh, on account of sin: He condemned sin in the flesh, that the righteous requirement of the law might be fulfilled in us who do not walk according to the flesh but according to the Spirit. For those who live according to the flesh set their minds on the

things of the flesh, but those who live according to the Spirit, the things of the Spirit. For to be carnally minded is death, but to be spiritually minded is life and peace. (Romans 7:18–8:6)

What the law wasn't able to do, God did. How? By sending Jesus Christ. What was the law unable to do? The law was unable to change you. Just like a mirror, it's unable to change you. A mirror doesn't have any power to change what it reveals. And the law had no power to change a person. It simply reveals, just like the law does today.

Laws really don't speak to people who don't break the law. It's when you break the law that the law yells at you and says, "You're a lawbreaker." Like when a police officer (like the one we talked about in Chapter 1) clocks you driving 65 miles per hour in a 25-mile-per-hour zone. He pulls you over and points out the black-and-white sign with 25 miles an hour on it. Even if you didn't see it, the law speaks. And it condemns you.

If you were going 25, the law wouldn't speak to you because you're not a lawbreaker. When you compare the sign to your speedometer and your speedometer matches the sign, there's comfort. There's no battle. But when the speedometer exceeds what the sign says, there's a great battle there.

For those of you who broke the law quite a bit before you were saved, you probably remember how you were always looking over your shoulder. You were constantly peeking around the corner, checking things out. But if you didn't break the law, you didn't care.

You feel the same way when it comes to the things of God. When you're walking in the Spirit, the Bible is alive to you. Your life matches the law, and you enjoy it.

But if you start sinfully speeding through life, you're uncomfortable with the law. You get upset with someone. And when you're reminded that the Bible says, "Be kind," you get mad at the Bible. Or you make an excuse about why you didn't need to be kind. You tell yourself they deserved it. When you do, you're taking the place of God and writing your own Bible.

Paul was struggling. He was wrestling. He described very much what we feel at times. *The things I want to do, I don't do. And the things I don't want to do, I do. What is going on?* The flesh. That's what's going on.

Just reading through Romans 7 can be exhausting. It reminds us of ourselves. You ask yourself, *What am I doing? What has happened to me? What kind of Christian life is this? What is it to follow Jesus? I'm trying. I'm trying.*

Somebody recently mentioned to me, "I'm trying." And my automatic response was, "No, there's no such thing as trying. Do it!" Trying is not doing, not yielding and abiding. It gets frustrating. It's a battle. You wonder, *Who's going to deliver me from this?*

In the midst of the struggle, remember what Paul shared. It gets exhausting because you can't win the battle in your own strength. You can't will yourself to win. You can't read enough self-help books or Bible studies. You can't do it. It's impossible.

It's impossible because God's standard is perfection. And no one is perfect. You're not perfect. And neither am I.

## *Jesus Delivers Us from the Law*

The key to the struggle is not *how* you get out of this, but *Who* will deliver you. When you're focused on the how, that's the law. But the Who? That's grace. And there's a big difference.

Too many Christians spend their lives asking how. "How do I get over this? How do I get through this? How?" But the real issue in your life isn't how, it's Who. Who will deliver you from this body of death? Who will come to your rescue? As long as you live your Christian life, clinging to the *how* question, you'll be spiritually exhausted. You'll be that wretched man.

I understand there's a place for instruction. The Bible speaks of discipleship. A regular part of Jesus' ministry was spent teaching. That's not what I'm referring to. I'm referring to those who are looking for a quick fix, who are just looking for the steps they need to follow.

If I gave you a list of the steps you should take based on the problem you have, you would be relieved. You'd think you had the solution in your hands. But it would be for the wrong reasons. Your relief wouldn't be based on your trust and faith in Jesus. It would be based on my experience as a Bible teacher. And that peace and comfort would only be temporary.

As you work through the list, you will fail. That's the problem with lists and rules and regulations.

Your desire for the steps—the manual—will not ultimately help you. Only God can do that work in you. It's the newness of the Spirit—Christ in you—not the oldness of the letter of the law, that brings life. That's the new covenant.

Who will deliver you? Christ in you, the hope of glory. Day by day, He's working in you. As Paul said, "I thank God—through Jesus Christ our Lord!" (Romans 7:25). Jesus is our deliverer. He lives in us and helps us from the inside. He strengthens us. He encourages us. He helps us to believe the promises of God!

That's something that I could never do for you. As a man of God—a fellow brother, a pastor, and a servant—I can never help you from the inside. Never. That's not the realm that God has given to me. I can't help you from the inside. I can only point you to the One who can. I can only remind you of His presence. I can only help you see His strength.

### A Picture of Grace in Noah's Life

Grace didn't appear for the first time in the New Testament. God is a God of grace. From the very beginning of creation, God demonstrated His grace to us. The grace of God—the scarlet thread of God's redemption through Jesus Christ—is all throughout the Bible. Let me show you a picture of it. It's so encouraging.

In Genesis 5, the Bible introduces us to a man named Noah. And then in the next chapter, we learn that "Noah found grace in the eyes of the LORD" (Genesis 6:8).

Noah found grace. How was Noah preserved from the judgment of God through the flood? He was preserved the same way you and I are preserved—by grace, through faith. It was a gift of God, not of works, lest anyone should boast (Ephesians 2:8–9). Noah is a great example. He found grace in the eyes of God. The grace of God saved Noah and his family from destruction.

In Genesis 6, Noah was given very specific instructions about how to build the ark. In those instructions, we are given a picture of God's grace. God told him, "Make yourself an ark of gopherwood; make rooms in the ark, and cover it inside and outside with pitch" (Genesis 6:14).

God instructed him to use pitch. The Hebrew word for pitch is koper.[1] The word is derived from the Hebrew word kapar,[2] which means atonement.

Atonement is a technical word that means forgiveness. It speaks of God's mercy in forgiving our sins. The way you can remember that word is to break it down into what it looks like: at . . . one . . . ment. The word atonement means that you and I are made one with God. We're brought into unity with God because our sins have been forgiven and the wrath of God is no longer upon us.

Noah was told to build a wooden ark. And he was to cover it with pitch. So, the ark becomes a picture and a type of the atonement of Jesus Christ. It's a picture of Jesus. The only way Noah and his family could be saved was to be *inside* the ark. That was God's instruction—for Noah and his family to go into the ark (Genesis 7:1). Get inside.

And the Bible says that the Lord shut the door (Genesis 7:16).

They didn't have to set up a pulley system. God shut them in. And for 40 days and 40 nights, the waters—the judgment of God —came down and began to rise. But Noah and his family were in the ark—covered, protected, and safe.

Aren't you glad that God told them to go inside the ark? In the instruction to make the ark, God *didn't* say,

*Okay, Noah, the storms are coming and the floods are coming and the destruction is coming. Here's what I want you to do: I want you to build the ark and put four pegs on each side. And for 40 days and 40 nights, you and your family need to hang on for dear life. If you hang on to the end, you'll be safe.*

God didn't say that. It wasn't about Noah's ability to hold on to a peg in order to be saved from judgment. It wasn't about his family's ability. You can sort of picture them holding on for a couple of hours. Or maybe they were super strong and could have made it eight hours. But they wouldn't have made it 40 days.

Thankfully, God didn't tell them to hold on for dear life. He had them go into the ark. And then He shut them in where they would be safe.

*The safest place for you to be is hidden in Christ.*

And God doesn't ask you to hold on for dear life either. No, He tells you, "Get inside. I'll shut you in. Do you want to be free from your past? Get inside." The safest place for you to be is hidden in Christ. Like the Bible says in Colossians 3:3, "For you died, and your life is hidden with Christ in God." You're hidden.

So many are trying to hold on—to stay away from sin. You may not realize it when you're saying this, but you hear this all the time. When you ask, "How are you doing today?" Many reply, "Hanging in there." You could stump them by asking, "Really, so you're hanging on to the pegs outside the ark?"

*Just hanging in there.* It's really a reflection that they're about to give in. When you use that vernacular—whether you mean it in a spiritual way or not—it's not about you hanging in there. It's about God's firm grip on your life. Even if you let go, God's holding on to you. As the Bible tells us, a righteous man may fall seven times, but he'll rise again (Proverbs 24:16). It's the faithfulness of God.

As we learned from Romans 8:1, there is therefore now no condemnation in Christ. That's where freedom from your past comes—to be in Christ and the freshness of His work. When the Father looks at you and me, He doesn't see us with all our failures and faults. Although He knows everything about us, He chooses to see us in Christ. Not only does Jesus come to live in you, but you're also put in Him. You're covered both ways.

### Grace Supersedes the Law

We have great freedom in Christ. According to Romans 8:2, the Spirit of life in Christ Jesus has made us free from the law of sin and death. What is the Spirit of life in Christ? It's the gospel. The good news is the freedom of the Spirit of life.

You see, the law wasn't done away with. The law shows us our need for Jesus. It's still doing its job. It's holy. It's just. And it's good. As we learn from Galatians 3:24, "the law was our tutor to bring us to Christ, that we might be justified by faith."

The law can refer to a number of things. It could be a reference to the ten commandments, the first five books of the Old Testament known as the Torah, or the Mosaic Covenant. It's the reality of God's demands upon our lives—His teachings and instructions to the Jewish people, revealing His desire for their purity. And the law tells you over and over again that you're a sinner and must surely die. That's the root of the law.

The law of sin and death is like the law of gravity. If you walk through the terminal at the airport, you'll see plane after plane, sitting there parked. Why? Because they're held down by gravity. But when the pilot gets ready, those same planes will be in flight. A new law supersedes gravity. The pilot starts up the plane, gets it running, and then the law of aerodynamics, with thrust and lift, take over.

Does that mean that the law of gravity goes away? No. It still has its job. And it still works perfectly.

So too with the law of sin and death. Grace supersedes that law. In Christ, you're no longer bound to it. In Christ, you're under the law of the Spirit of life. Jesus set us free from the law of sin and death. We're free to live for Jesus by faith.

Remember the people who went to Jesus and asked Him, "What shall we do, that we may work the works of God?" (John 6:28). That's a common question asked today. People want something they can do. We're tethered to the law, motivated by it, striving to attain it, and working hard to please God. But listen carefully to Jesus' answer. He said, "This is the work of God, that you believe in Him whom He sent" (John 6:29).

We are free—not by working hard or doing more. Not by following rules and regulations. And not by dressing right, using the right language, having perfect devotions, or reading through the Bible a million times. It's by faith. We are made free by faith. The Spirit of life that lives in you draws you away from the law of sin and death. You're not bound by it any longer.

I love Romans 8:3, "For what the law could not do in that it was weak through the flesh, God did by sending His own Son." The law cannot give life. It cannot give power. The law has no ability to forgive. Forgiveness only comes from God through Jesus Christ. That's the only way it comes. What the law couldn't do, God did. How? By sending Jesus Christ to die for you and me.

Living by God's grace sets you free from the past. It gives you freedom. The law is weak because it can't change your flesh. Your inability to keep the law reveals its weakness. The law can't change you from the inside out. You can't follow enough rules and lists. You can't read enough books to make you right with God.

If you're still not convinced, you can write your goals on index cards and post them all over your house. But the only thing you'll see every time you see those cards is your weakness and inability to follow them. Because if you had the strength to follow them, you wouldn't need a reminder on the mirror.

It's good to be reminded. That's not the issue. But every time we need to be reminded, all it does is reveal your weakness. Your inability to remember everything shows your weakness, not your strength.

And even if you post a card, telling yourself, *I will be a good person today, the best person I could ever be*—even if you put one on the mirror, on your shoes, in your car, and you memorize it— what a burden you've placed on yourself. Of course, it's good to be good. But every day—that little goal—you'll have to be better than you were the day before, or you've failed. If Monday was your best day, when you wake up on Tuesday, you're going to have to be even better.

Or maybe you set the bar so low that you can hit it. But then you feel guilty because you know that wasn't your best.

Another thing we do is set up rules and regulations that you can do but others can't. Let me put it this way. Have you noticed that your sin looks really bad in someone else's life? You seem to notice certain sins in other people's lives. And you seem shocked by them. You may even say, "I can't believe she did that." But then, over time, God reveals that the sin you've been noticing in others' lives is the sin that you need to deal with in your own life.

There's an example of this in the Bible. David's friend came to him with a story. The Lord sent Nathan to David, and Nathan told him a story. He said,

There were two men in one city, one rich and the other poor. The rich man had exceedingly many flocks and herds. But the poor man had nothing, except one little ewe lamb which he had bought and nourished; and it grew up together with him and with his children. It ate of his own food and drank from his own cup and lay in his bosom; and it was like a daughter to him. And a traveler came to the rich man, who refused to take from his own flock and from his own herd to prepare one for the wayfaring man who had come to him; but he took the poor man's lamb and prepared it for the man who had come to him. (2 Samuel 12:1–4)

It was a great injustice, and David got angry. And what did David pronounce against the rich man in that story? Death. David said, "As the LORD lives, the man who has done this shall surely die!" (2 Samuel 12:5).

The death penalty wasn't even appropriate for the crime. The penalty would have been to give back a couple of lambs.

But what was on David's mind? The death penalty. Why? Because he was a murderer. David had committed adultery and then had the woman's husband killed to cover up his sin (2 Samuel 11).

You see, the law doesn't bring you freedom. Only Jesus Christ can do that. God did what the law couldn't do. He sent His own Son to die for you. And by faith in Jesus, freedom is yours. By faith in Him, you fulfill all the requirements of the law.

If you want to be free from your past, you need to be in Christ. Jesus does the work. He empowers, helps, and strengthens you. Along with His command, Jesus gives you the power to fulfill it.

As the Bible instructs us,

And we have such trust through Christ toward God. Not that we are sufficient of ourselves to think of anything as being from ourselves, but our sufficiency is from God. (2 Corinthians 3:4–5)

That's the language of grace. We have nothing to offer. Our sufficiency is in Christ. It's from God.

[God] made us sufficient as ministers of the new covenant, not of the letter but of the Spirit; for the letter kills, but the Spirit gives life.

But if the ministry of death, written and engraved on stones, was glorious, so that the children of Israel could not look steadily at the face of Moses because of the glory of his countenance, which glory was passing away, how will the ministry of the Spirit not be more glorious? For if the ministry of condemnation had glory, the ministry of righteousness exceeds much more in glory. For even what was made glorious had no glory in this respect, because of the glory that excels. For if what is passing away was glorious, what remains is much more glorious. (2 Corinthians 3:6–11)

So, let's look at the contrast:

- The Old Covenant is the law of sin and death. The New Covenant is the law of the Spirit of life.
- The Old Covenant is the ministry of death. But the New Covenant is the ministry of life.
- The Old Covenant was written on stones. It was external. It was demanding. It had this external, outward change in conformity to a list. But the New Covenant is actually written on hearts, as promised in Jeremiah 31 and Ezekiel 36.

God promised to do a work in the hearts of men. God gives

us a new nature. It's an internal change where you now desire to do the will of God. You don't desire to follow a list.

Ladies, it doesn't make you any more righteous if you cover your ankles. There's a whole system of theology asserting that the way you dress makes you more spiritual. The Bible speaks of modesty for men and women, for sure. But whether you cover your ankles or not, you're fine.

The external is not what God is looking for—it's the internal work of His Spirit. The Old Covenant was temporary. Its glory faded away. But the New Covenant is eternal in glory and righteousness. The Old Covenant was condemnation. But the New Covenant gives justification and the forgiveness of sins.

How are we set free from the past? Through God's Spirit who dwells in us. And here's the thing, your inability to let go of the past is a reflection of your own human effort. In your own effort, you have subjected yourself to the law of sin and death. But when you choose to obey God—when you release yourself to the law of the Spirit of life—you are instantly free.

Now you may go back. You may go back to the law of sin and death. But you can live in freedom again when you choose to believe what God has promised you in Romans 8. Don't go back to Romans 7 where you're under the law of sin and death. When you read through the book of Romans, you'll notice the progression of victory and joy.

I pray you'll recognize that God is the One who will set you free. It's not by your own effort. When we try to do things in our own effort, we make things worse, not better. And we delay the enjoyment of the very presence of God in our lives.

Instead, it's by faith, trusting in God's empowerment. It's by believing that God did what He said He's done. And it's by trusting that God will do what He said He'll do. Freedom will come as you surrender your life to Him.

# CHAPTER THREE

## Dealing With Your Past

E veryone has a past—a past that's been touched by sin. People have hurt you. And you've likely done things you regret.

What comes to mind when you think about your past? Is there something you wish wasn't a part of your testimony? Is there something you wish would disappear or that you could wipe clean?

That's where Romans 8:1 comes into our lives. Because no matter what comes to mind, there is therefore now no condemnation for those who are in Christ—your past included. There is no condemnation for your past.

However, in living with the reality of a past, the question remains—and it's a good, Biblical question: What is to be done with your past? You forget, forgive, and forsake it.

### Forgetting Your Past

First, you forget your past. As Paul told us,

> Not that I have already attained, or am already perfected; but I press on, that I may lay hold of that for which Christ Jesus has also laid hold of me. Brethren, I do not count myself to have apprehended; but one thing I do, *forgetting* those things which are behind and reaching forward to those things which are ahead, I press toward the goal for the prize of the upward call of God in Christ Jesus. (Philippians 3:12–14 (emphasis added))

Forgetting those things that are behind you, press forward. Now, I know this sounds too simplistic. But it's only simplistic if you approach it that way. Remember, you're not actually trying to erase a memory. Instead, it's a conscious choice to move forward. We forget the past by releasing the past and reaching for the future.

*We forget the past by releasing the past and reaching for the future.*

You can't reach forward if you're still holding on to the past. You won't make progress if you choose to look backward.

When you drive your car, aren't you amazed at how big your windshield is? It's huge compared to your rearview mirror. Do you usually drive your car in reverse—you know, by looking in your little rearview mirror? Or do they ever make a car with a windshield that's the size of a rearview mirror, so you only have a small area to see where you're going? Of course not. Because the best way to drive a car is forward.

You won't get very far if you're always looking in your rearview mirror. It's only a matter of time before you'll crash and hurt yourself and others.

You see, the first thing is to forget the past. You make a conscious choice to forget the past and remember that God has forgiven you.

Your past is going to come up over and over again. You're going to bring it up. Others will bring it up. Memories will come into your mind. And each time it does, you need to decide to forget it. Choose not to dwell in the past anymore.

I've found that the only time I can't seem to forget my past is when I choose to dwell in it. Can you relate to that? When I dwell in the past, I'm choosing to remember it. I make a decision to hang out and think about it for a while. You know how it goes —you start thinking about it, and then you start to drown in the sorrow and grief that it brings. You forget all that God has done. And before you know it, you're finished.

Choose to forget the past. Don't dwell on it. Yes, it was painful. You were hurt. But it's in the past. It's over. It's done.

Paul said, "I forget those things in the past, and I press on. I press toward the goal." The phrase *press on* means to run swiftly.[1] The idea is moving fast and going after it. That's what Paul did, he ran swiftly away from his past and swiftly toward the goal of Jesus Christ.

You have to forget the past. Although you may think you can't—in Christ, you can.

When I share my testimony, I do so not as an anchor in my life, but in light of the reality of what God has delivered me from. My past has a perspective now. I'm not proud of it. Nor do I choose to dwell on it. But if God can use the delivering power that He's demonstrated in my life, I will continue to share my testimony for the sake of deliverance in others' lives.

I can't help but think that someone reading this is in great bondage. When you're in great bondage, you don't believe that you'll be delivered. You can't see the possibility. You don't even have a concept of how life could be different—until someone comes along and shows you.

That's what happened to me. I remember it distinctly. I was listening to the testimony of Pastor Raul Ries. I can still remember where I was sitting and the sound of his voice. And I remember the freedom that was spoken into my life through the Word of God and through a man who was worse than me.

His testimony was where I was headed if God hadn't intervened. As I listened, I thought, *Man, if God can do that to this guy, then maybe* . . . . I didn't fully believe it. But it put me on the path of thinking that God could do that in my life. And it gave me hope.

The worst counselor in your life is actually not a friend. It's not that person who may be giving you bad advice. The worst counselor in your life tends to be you.

Did you know that you talk to yourself more than anyone? And that's not a weird thing. We all reason with ourselves and think through things. We have discussions with ourselves that are in no way unhealthy.

But when you go into that mode, you have to make a choice. Either you'll counsel yourself with the Word of God and His truths or with your own understanding. And we make great mistakes when we talk to ourselves without the Word of God open or the Word of God speaking to us.

You have to forget the past. I've found that the only time I can forget my past is when I choose to dwell on my future. I can't think about two things at the same time.

When I'm meditating on the Scriptures day and night, like God told Joshua to do (Joshua 1:8), I find myself enraptured in the potential of what God wants to do in my life. But if I dwell on some of the current circumstances in my life or something that happened yesterday, last week, or five and a half years ago, then I'm sunk.

Have you ever been there? Depression, discouragement, sorrow, and feeling sorry for yourself are always just one decision away. And those things are not from the Lord. They come from a weight of condemnation, a choice to reject God's will for your life. When you choose to play your past over and over again in your mind, it will bury you.

It's tempting to replay your past. Maybe you had an argument with someone. You replay the argument and think of all the things you said or could have said. You think, *Oh man, I could've said that.* But you can't say those things now nor choose not to say what you did because it's over.

The reality is that those who choose not to forget, tend to stay in one place their whole lives. That place of hurt or failure. That's where they're stuck. When you talk to them, that's what they talk about. Everyone around them has moved on, but they've chosen not to move forward.

If that's you, stop living in the past. Don't misunderstand me. I realize that things happen in life that are extremely painful. I know some of you have been violated and greatly hurt. Some of you have done great damage to your minds and your bodies. But Jesus is cleansing, washing, and changing you. He's redeemed you. And whatever happened is over. You're not there anymore.

When we're in Christ, there's no condemnation for us or for others. But the enemy's trap has been set. And it's always there to take you back.

I know some of you reading this are wrestling with me. You're battling this concept, this truth of forgetting and moving forward. You're arguing with me. And you might even be thinking, *Ed, you just don't understand. If you would be in my shoes for a week, you would understand.*

Well, I have to admit that I don't fully understand your pain, your problems, or your thoughts. I don't. So, there's no need to argue with me over that. I don't understand every problem in everyone's life. And that's really good news—that our freedom doesn't depend on our understanding.

I think I have a deeper empathy these days—a deeper compassion for people's pain and problems. But my empathy will only help you get to Jesus Christ. You see, it's not whether I understand or not. If I understood the way you understood, I'd probably hurt the way you hurt. And I'd probably face the same temptations you're facing. I'd be sitting in your seat.

The answer for all of us is the same. Jesus Christ has come to forgive us of all our sins, so we can forgive others and be free. He's forgiven us, so we can live a life that honors and pleases Him.

It's okay if you argue with me. But it's a waste of time. We often get defensive when the truth starts to get close. Defensiveness is always a sign that something's touched you. It's self-protection.

But aren't you tired of self-protecting and dealing with the same issue over and over again? Aren't you yearning and hoping for a better day? A better week? A better month? It's available to you now, in Christ.

The root of condemnation in a believer's life is always tied to looking back. After all, what would the enemy condemn you about from the future? You don't even know what the future is yet. It hasn't been lived out.

The root of condemnation is always the past. You can't be condemned when you're looking upward and forward. That's why the enemy loves for you to look back on the past and keep your eyes focused on the sin—your sin or someone else's. The enemy knows, if he can get people to look back on the past, many of them will stay right there.

For that reason, I'm guarded, even in what I share with you. I don't want to go back to the past. And I don't want to stay there. But I have to say, many of the regrets in my life were the old Ed. And the good news is that the Bible says the old Ed is dead. That's the way it is. I'm a new creation in Christ (2 Corinthians 5:17).

Condemnation is rooted in the past. For those of you fighting this, let me ask you: Are you really choosing to stay in your past? Do you know how many people stay in the past, live in the past, and never discover the future or enjoy the presence of the Lord?

Your future is literally just a few feet ahead. It's just one decision away. Let go of the past. God is telling you to let go. He's telling you to move on. Because you are free in Christ.

## *Forgiving Your Past*

Next, in dealing with your past, you need to forgive it. Forgive your past. Forgiveness is the key to a healthy, vibrant life in Christ.

I want you to learn something from Jesus in Luke 15. It's a very familiar story.

> A certain man had two sons. And the younger of them said to his father, "Father, give me the portion of goods that falls to me." So he divided to them his livelihood. (Luke 15:11–12)

What did the son do exactly? By asking for his inheritance early, the son, in effect, said to his dad, "I wish you were dead. I don't want the kind of relationship that we have today. I want what is mine—as if you were dead. When you die, I get all of this. But I want it now."

The son was truly separated from his dad at this point. His heart was full of selfishness. And his dad gave it to him. So, let's see what the son did with the inheritance.

> And not many days after, the younger son gathered all together, journeyed to a far country, and there wasted his possessions with prodigal living. (Luke 15:13)

The son chose to live a sinful life. He left Israel. He left the comfort of his home and his family. He literally left his senses.

Look at the verbs used in that verse—the son gathered; he journeyed; and he wasted. That's what sin will do to you. It will waste you. It brings you to a place where you don't want to be.

You might be deciding whether to do something in your life that has two paths. One is a holy choice that you could make unto the Lord. The other requires a little compromise. If you choose the compromise, as you gather and journey, you're going to waste at least a portion of your life. You might waste a day or two, a month, or a couple of years. But it will be a waste. And if you've already compromised, you can repent and turn from it right now. Don't waste any more time.

That's what the son did. He wasted everything. He took all that his dad had given him and wasted it.

> But when he had spent all, there arose a severe famine in that land, and he began to be in want. Then he went and joined himself to a citizen of that country, and he sent him into his fields to feed swine. And he would gladly have filled his stomach with the pods that the swine ate, and no one gave him anything. (Luke 15:14–16)

The son began to be in want. The world will never satisfy you. Have you noticed that? And then the son was in need. He was so hungry; he was willing to eat the pigs' food.

And then the son finally came to his senses.

> But when he came to himself, he said, "How many of my father's hired servants have bread enough and to spare, and I perish with hunger! I will arise and go to my father, and will say to him, 'Father, I have sinned against heaven and before you, and I am no longer worthy to be called your son. Make me like one of your hired servants.'" (Luke 15:17–19)

It says that "he came to himself." When he did, he returned home to his father.

Some of you may be praying for prodigal sons and daughters in your lives today. You need to pray that they will come to the end of themselves. And it might become a prayer like, "Whatever it takes, Lord. I want them to recognize and realize that where they're at now is not Your best for them. Whatever it takes to bring them home."

And he arose and came to his father. But when he was still a great way off, his father saw him and had compassion, and ran and fell on his neck and kissed him. And the son said to him, "Father, I have sinned against heaven and in your sight, and am no longer worthy to be called your son." (Luke 15:20–21)

I know we call this the parable of the prodigal son. But if you took a pen and circled every time the word father is mentioned, I think you would agree with me that it's actually the parable of the loving father. A father who had *two* sons.

The father ran toward his repentant son and received him. He didn't even wait for the son to come all the way back. He had probably been looking down that road every single day. And the moment he saw his son, he ran to him.

He had already forgiven him. The father was ready to forgive before he even talked to his son. He didn't wait for his son to explain everything. He was running to his son as soon as he recognized that he had come home.

Isn't that a great picture of our heavenly Father? When you turn back to Jesus, that's what the Father does in your life. He runs to you. He doesn't wait for you to come all the way. He's not standing there with His arms crossed in anger. Our God is full of love, mercy, and compassion. When you turn back after days, months, or years of prodigal living, He runs to you with compassion.

> *When you turn back to Jesus, that's what the Father does in your life. He runs to you.*

However, the son's still condemning himself. He says, "Father, I have sinned against heaven and in your sight, and am no longer worthy to be called your son" (Luke 15:21). The son felt unworthy. He was under self-condemnation.

But look at what the father did. The father told his servants,

"Bring out the best robe and put it on him, and put a ring on his hand and sandals on his feet. And bring the fatted calf here and kill it, and let us eat and be merry; for this my son was dead and is alive again; he was lost and is found." And they began to be merry. (Luke 15:22–24)

That sounds like a great end to the story, right? Everything's wonderful. The prodigal son was back, and he repented. He's changed. He's learned. He's washed and cleansed. He's not a servant; he's a son. And there's forgiveness from the father.

Yet, not everyone was so willing to forgive.

Now his older son was in the field. And as he came and drew near to the house, he heard music and dancing. So he called one of the servants and asked what these things meant. And he said to him, "Your brother has come, and because he has received him safe and sound, your father has killed the fatted calf."

But he was angry and would not go in. Therefore his father came out and pleaded with him. So he answered and said to his father, "Lo, these many years I have been serving you; I never transgressed your commandment at any time; and yet you never gave me a young goat, that I might make merry with my friends. But as soon as this son of yours came, who has devoured your livelihood with harlots, you killed the fatted calf for him."

And he said to him, "Son, you are always with me, and all that I have is yours. It was right that we should make merry and be glad, for your brother was dead and is alive again, and was lost and is found." (Luke 15:25–32)

The older son represents condemnation in this parable. He had been faithfully working. He had a relationship with his dad and enjoyed all the comforts and blessings of being with his dad. But he represents condemnation.

I want you to notice that condemnation is not just rooted in your past. It's rooted in unforgiveness. Unforgiveness leads to condemnation.

If you're condemned, you're not receiving the forgiveness that's available in Christ. And if you're condemning others, like the older son, then you're not extending that forgiveness. And it's a sad, twisted way to live a life that passes so quickly.

People who are bitter immediately pull you into their past offenses. They say something like, "Well, did you hear about what this person did to me?" And you're like, "No, did it happen right now?" "No, no, but they probably did it to you too. They probably . . . ." If this sounds like you, you need to forgive and you need to move on.

The Bible says that we need to forgive one another (Colossians 3:13). That's what will release you from bitterness. Do you want to be released? Forgive . . . and forgive . . . and forgive. But when you choose not to forgive, you become stuck in your hurt, your pain, or your failure.

Those who choose not to forgive are pretty obvious. They stay in one place, unwilling to move forward. They have a tendency to whine and complain, tainting every relationship they have. Just like the Bible says, the root of bitterness defiles many (Hebrews 12:15). Unfortunately, it's common in the body of Christ.

If you're in the son's place, coming back to your Dad, you can't bring your past with you. And you can't do anything to change your past. You come to Him broken because of your past. You need to learn how to live in your Father's favor because the Father forgives the repentant.

Isn't that a wonderful thought? The Father forgives the repentant. And you wouldn't be repentant if it wasn't for the work of the Spirit of God in your life. So it's a work that begins with Him and ends with Him. And we get to be a part of it.

The very fact that you want to say you're sorry is His Spirit convicting you, calling you, and drawing you into the future, not the past. And the day that you say, "I'm sick of my sin, and I hate it," is the day when you agree with the working, convicting, finished work of Jesus Christ in your life.

But realize, there's always the big brother. You're relieved. You're free. You come home, and Dad's there. But so is your big brother. Dad is the picture of forgiveness. And the big brother of condemnation.

The big brother doesn't even need to be another person. The big brother could be your head. Why? Because, at times, we're unwilling to receive God's forgiveness. Let me put it a different way. Sometimes you refuse to forgive yourself.

Now I know the world's twisted that idea. The world will tell you that you can't love others until you love yourself. The problem is you love yourself too much. That's the problem. And that raises up pride.

When the world says to forgive yourself, they speak of pampering yourself, taking care of yourself, and putting yourself first. They tell you that you're the most important person. So, make sure that you take care of yourself before you take care of anyone else. That's not a Biblical definition.

The need to forgive yourself is rooted in the truth of receiving the forgiveness of God. It's not an act of power on your part but a choice to surrender, in accepting God's forgiveness.

Some of you may be thinking, *But Ed, you don't understand what I did*. And perhaps I don't. But I can assure you that God does. And He loves you. And He sent His Son Jesus Christ to die for you. So, when you forgive yourself, it's simply believing what God says about you.

There is no condemnation. The price has been paid by Jesus. And the anger, bitterness, and frustration you feel will leave when you accept God's forgiveness for your past. Receive His forgiveness so you're able to move on.

When you choose not to accept forgiveness for your own failures, that's called idolatry. You become a little god in your life. When you refuse to accept forgiveness, you're, in effect, saying, "I understand that God forgave me. But if I was God, I wouldn't forgive myself. So I'll become God and hold it against myself the rest of my life."

The release from the cycle of condemnation is surrender—agreeing that God has forgiven you in Christ Jesus. Accept and receive His forgiveness.

The God of the universe who created you—He loves you and sent His Son Jesus Christ to die for you. God forgives the repentant. And what's left for us to do but simply say, thank you.

If the Father runs to embrace you, what do you do? You take the hug. And it feels good. As you're embraced, you just kind of think, *I can't believe this is happening. After everything I did to Him and everything I've done.*

Despite what the son did—the damage to his relationship with his dad by asking for the inheritance and then wasting his dad's money on sinful living—his dad not only ran to embrace him; he threw him a party.

And with all that, the father said, "It was right that we should make merry and be glad, for your brother was dead and is alive again, and was lost and is found" (Luke 15:32). It's right to forgive the past and receive forgiveness.

So many want to focus on the bad, on the negative. In the sanctuary of our church, we have offering boxes. Those boxes are for the sole purpose of tithes, offerings, and prayer requests. But some people who visit here actually think that they are complaint boxes. They don't offer a tithe or an offering. They offer a complaint about how they don't like the carpet or couldn't find a parking space. They're in a place where God wants to minister to them, and their eyes are on the carpet. There are just people like that.

But when there's repentance, we should be focused on the forgiveness we receive from the Father. The world will tell you that it's all about you. But God says, "No, it's not about you. It's about My Son, Jesus."

The enemy loves to get our eyes off the main thing. And sometimes we gladly cooperate. Don't get distracted from what's important. Keep your eyes on Jesus and keep forgetting and forgiving your past. It's a decision you'll need to continually make.

If you hear a song that reminds you of your past, choose to forget and forgive it. If you see something on social media that brings your past front and center in your mind, choose to forget and forgive it. Make a conscious choice to focus on Jesus. Tell yourself, *I'm not going back there. I've been freed in Jesus Christ. I'm looking forward.*

God will help you to receive the embrace of the Father—to receive His love and forgiveness—and to keep your focus on Him.

### Forsaking Your Past

After forgetting your past and forgiving your past, you should forsake your past.

The Bible gives us very practical instructions for life. I want you to trust the Bible. It's not only God's love letter to you, revealing a loving, caring God. It's also God's manual for living life.

And in Psalm 103, we learn about God's heart toward us as born-again believers. It says,

> Bless the LORD, O my soul; and all that is within me, bless His holy name!

Bless the LORD, O my soul, and forget not all His benefits: who forgives all your iniquities, who heals all your diseases, who redeems your life from destruction, who crowns you with lovingkindness and tender mercies, who satisfies your mouth with good things, so that your youth is renewed like the eagle's.

The LORD executes righteousness and justice for all who are oppressed. He made known His ways to Moses, His acts to the children of Israel.

The LORD is merciful and gracious, slow to anger, and abounding in mercy. He will not always strive with us, nor will He keep His anger forever. He has not dealt with us according to our sins, nor punished us according to our iniquities. (Psalm 103:1–10)

At this point in the psalm, you should just say a hearty amen. I remember a conversation I had with someone about justice. When you feel injustice, you often have this thought of wanting justice for the other person.

Yet, when it comes to yourself, you don't want justice, do you? I know I don't want justice. I don't ask God for justice for the wrongs I've committed. If I did, I'd be judged according to my iniquities and my failures. I don't want justice. I want Jesus.

I want Jesus for me. And I should want Jesus for others. Even those who have hurt me or are hurting me. I want Jesus to heal and change. I don't want justice.

And in Psalm 103, God's heart toward us is not justice. He has not dealt with us according to our sins. He has not punished us according to our iniquities. Not only that, but as you continue reading Psalm 103, you'll see an amazing thing.

For as the heavens are high above the earth, so great is His mercy toward those who fear Him; as far as the east is from the west, so far has He removed our transgressions from us.

As a father pities his children, so the LORD pities those who fear Him. For He knows our frame; He remembers that we are dust. (Psalm 103:11–14)

As born-again believers, God forgives and forsakes our sins because Jesus paid the penalty for them on the cross. And we need to receive His forgiveness and forsake them too. The word forsake literally means to let it go; to let it sink or drop. God forsakes our sins.

On the other hand, the Bible says over and over that God will not forsake *you*. Jesus will never leave or forsake you (*see, e.g.,* Hebrews 13:5). So when we think of that word, God will never let you sink. He'll never drop you.

The Lord is merciful and gracious, slow to anger, and abounding in mercy. He doesn't treat us as our sin deserves. Instead, He says, "I'll forgive you. I'll throw it. I'll cast it. I'll drive your sin away." That's what the word remove means in Psalm 103:12.[2] God casts our sin as far as the east is from the west.

Forsake your past. Let it sink. Let it drop. Stop letting the past be an excuse for your inactivity today.

*Let it go. Let it sink. Let God begin to do a work.*

I know some of you have experienced horrendous things. Painful things. But I'm so thankful they're in the past. They're over. It's done. Even if they happened when you weren't a Christian, God was for you. He was tenderly loving you, drawing you to Himself, washing you, and changing you. God took away that little root of bitterness and comforted you in your pain. He gave you that one good night's sleep or that good week or month of rest and calm. And then the month became a year.

Yet, the enemy always wants you to use the past as an excuse for inactivity today. Don't do that. The past isn't holding you back. But you might be holding on to your past. Let it go. Let it sink. Let God begin to do a work.

You know, it's like a child with a toy. In the nursery, we have toys. And when the kids get ahold of a toy, they become superhuman. Sometimes, you have to pry their fingers off of it. As soon as you get one finger off, they grab the toy again. They won't let go.

And some of you are holding on to your past. The Holy Spirit's trying to pry your fingers off of it. Let go. Let it sink. Forsake it.

It's a little different than forgetting, isn't it? Forgetting is in the mind. Forsaking is in the life. It's where you say, "I'm letting it go. I'm letting it sink. I'm not going to hold on to it any longer."

When you forsake your past, you let it sink into the sea of forgetfulness. You let it drop. You let it go. It's back there. And you're right here in the present.

As we've already learned, there is therefore now no condemnation (Romans 8:1). Right now. For those who walk in the Spirit, the Spirit walk is forward. It's progressive. It's spiritually alive. But the flesh walk, the condemnation walk is regressive, backward, and spiritually dead.

## God Enables You to Forget, Forgive, and Forsake

You may think it's impossible to forget, forgive, and forsake your past. But God is into the impossible. What's impossible with man is possible with God. And the commands of God always come with His enablement to follow through.

I know some of you reading this may be overwhelmed by even the possibility. Some of you are in a spiritual prison—or even a physical one. If you're physically locked up, you know you did something you wish you hadn't done. You've got a mark on your record. And you just sit there thinking it's impossible to follow through with what you have before you.

But even in a spiritual prison, you feel shackled and held back. You feel like there's no future.

Listen, the power of God is greater than your inability. As a pastor, all I can do is teach you the Bible—lay it before you, encourage you, and exhort you. It's up to you to act on it.

If you believe it and do it, crazy, wonderful changes will take place in your life. You will be spiritually free. But if you sit around—upset and arguing with the pastor, with the Bible, and ultimately with God—you're going to stay in the same place. And it's going to get worse. The wages of sin is always death. You can't escape it.

So, let me show you an example of how God enables you when you step out in faith to do what He commands you to do. There was a man with a withered hand who had an encounter with Jesus in Luke 6.

> Now it happened on another Sabbath, also, that He entered the synagogue and taught. And a man was there whose right hand was withered. So the scribes and Pharisees watched Him closely, whether He would heal on the Sabbath, that they might find an accusation against Him. But He knew their thoughts, and said to the man who had the withered hand, "Arise and stand here." And he arose and stood. (Luke 6:6–8)

Now, first of all, I think God is very gracious to this man, telling him to do something that he could actually do. Get up and come over here. And he had to process that for a second. But you know how fast your mind works. *My legs are fine; I can stand up and walk.* Boom, it happens that fast. And he did what Jesus told him to do.

And that's how it is with you too. There are so many things in your life that you have no problem doing. Get up Sunday morning, come to church. Study the Word. Pray. Read the Bible. Share the gospel. And you say, "Yes, yes, yes. I can do that. I can do all those things. I'll be at church. I'll read." And you listen. And it's just wonderful. It's so joyous.

Jesus tells you, "Arise and stand here." And you think, *No problem. I'll get up and stand. I'll come to you, Jesus. No problem. I don't have any problem with that at all. I can do that.*

But then He says, "Okay, I want you to forget your past. I want you to forgive your past. I want you to forsake your past." And you tell yourself, *I can't do that.*

So, let's see what else Jesus asked the man to do.

Then Jesus said to them, "I will ask you one thing: Is it lawful on the Sabbath to do good or to do evil, to save life or to destroy?" And when He had looked around at them all, He said to the man, "Stretch out your hand." (Luke 6:9–10)

Do you know what that was? An impossibility. He couldn't stretch out his hand. It was withered. I mean, you've got to understand the weight of this.

And that's how you might be feeling with the idea of forgetting, forgiving, and forsaking your past. You might be thinking, *It's impossible. I'll come to church. I'll read the Bible. I'll love God and serve Him. Keep telling me things I can do. Don't tell me to do what I can't do.*

Some of you argue or wrestle with truth. It's hard for you to receive it. It takes a little time. Maybe you're like Jesus' disciple, Thomas. Thomas needed more time. He had to see something. He had to feel something. And Jesus was so gracious. He said, "You want to see the wound in my side? Put your hand in there, bro. Go ahead. Do whatever you gotta do. Like, this is true. You want to see my wounds? Great" (John 20:24–27 (my paraphrase)). I'm grateful he didn't rebuke Thomas. He gave him what he needed.

Yet here, with the man with the withered hand, the next sentence says, "And he did so" (Luke 6:10). Jesus told the man, "Stretch out your hand." Then there's a quotation mark, a space, and the word "and." In that space, the man could've said, "No way. This guy doesn't know what He's talking about. My hand's been withered forever. Look at it. It doesn't move. I haven't moved this hand for years. This is impossible. I won't do it."

It could've been in there. It's not in there, but it could've been. There could have been another sentence. Or a whole paragraph telling us about the faithlessness of this man. But notice what it says, not what it doesn't say. It says,

"Stretch out your hand." And he did so. (Luke 6:10)

What do you mean, he did so? His hand was withered. So think of this, there's no pause. Stretch out your hand; he did so. Just like that. Why? Because with the command—in the breath of the command of God—comes His enabling power for you to do what He tells you to do. It's not your strength. It's not your wisdom. It's your faith that makes you well.

This is powerful for us. In those times when hope is withering up like this hand—when you're paralyzed and struggling—know this: As Jesus enters in, He's always drawn toward the one who's hurting the most. He's not so interested in the mockers, the game players, and the ones who want to test Him. Jesus knows your thoughts.

The fact that Jesus knows your thoughts right now could make you feel good or uneasy. But He's always on the lookout for the one who's hurting the most. And He found this man. He gave the command. And it was an absolute impossibility for the man to do this. He must have tried to send the signal from his brain to his hand a million times before.

I don't know if you've ever lived with something that's so hurtful, painful, and difficult that it's on your mind the second you wake up. It's on your mind when you fall asleep. Sometimes it's so pervasive that you dream about it. You can't even get away from it in your sleep.

No doubt the disability in this man's life was something that was always on his mind. And sure, he must have resolved that he would live his life with what he had. But that doesn't mean he didn't deal with it every day.

So when Jesus gave him the command, he could've said no. But he didn't. He decided to obey. And just like the man, as you purpose in your heart to obey, God will meet you in that place. Let it be your story that when God says to you, "Forget, forgive, and forsake your past," the next sentence is, "And she did so." "And he did so."

If you choose to obey, God will show up in a powerful way. The moment that God commands an impossible thing, He'll enable you to follow through.

Although the past keeps coming back, don't hold on to it. Let it go. Forget the past. Don't bring it back or dwell on it. Forgive the past, both enjoying the forgiveness of the Father and extending the forgiveness of the Father. Forsake the past, letting it go, leaving it behind.

We need to obey God—to step out in faith—to forget our past, forgive our past, and forsake our past. Release your past and move forward. As you make that decision of obedience, little by little, the Holy Spirit will affirm that in your life and strengthen you. Whether it's your recent past or a distant one, God's life-giving power will enable you.

# CHAPTER FOUR

## Dealing With Forgiveness

A number of years ago in a small town in Spain, a man and his teenage son had a very painful argument. The argument led to a falling out between them. Deep feelings of bitterness, resentment, and unforgiveness followed. The son launched out on his own, angry and upset. He left his home in the countryside and went to the city.

As time passed, the father regretted it. He sensed the mistakes he had made and how he had treated his son. So, he searched for his boy, day and night. Several months passed, and he still wasn't able to find him. In one last-ditch effort, he placed the following ad in the classified section of the Madrid newspaper:

*Dear Paco, Meet me in front of the newspaper office at noon. All is forgiven. I love you. Your father.*

By twelve o'clock the next day, there were over 800 men named Paco gathered outside the newspaper building. Every one of them was looking for forgiveness from his father.[1]

There's a desperate need for forgiveness today. If such an

advertisement was put out on Facebook or Instagram with your name on it, saying forgiveness is available, would you show up looking for the forgiveness that you never received?

In the last chapter, we learned how important it is to forgive your past—how you need to forgive yourself by accepting God's forgiveness. Another component of forgiving your past is to forgive others.

Forgiveness is so needed. Families are broken. Marriages are dissolved. Painful circumstances continue to happen, resulting in separation and division. It's a hard time. The Bible warned us: In the last days, the hearts of many will grow cold (Matthew 24:12). And that includes believers. It's possible for our hearts to grow cold and hard toward the things of God.

When you hold on to resentment, anger, and bitterness, you're living with an unforgiving spirit. Unforgiveness continues to weaken the Church, divide families, and erode the effectiveness of believers' lives. Damage, pain, and separation are rooted in the sin of unforgiveness. And yes, the Bible declares it to be a sin.

### Four Reasons You Should Forgive

Jesus taught His followers, "If you forgive those who sin against you, your heavenly Father will forgive you. But if you refuse to forgive others, your Father will not forgive your sins" (Matthew 6:14–15 (NLT)).

The forgiveness of others is non-negotiable. It's not a choice for the believer. Jesus told us to forgive as we've been forgiven. If you aren't convinced, here are four reasons you must forgive.[2]

1 **Forgiveness is commanded by God.**
Forgiveness is a command. And obedience isn't optional. Jesus instructed us in Matthew 6:14–15 to forgive. He

taught the same thing in Mark 11. Jesus said, "But when you are praying, first forgive anyone you are holding a grudge against, so that your Father in heaven will forgive your sins, too" (Mark 11:25 (NLT)). It's a command.

## 2 Forgiveness reflects Jesus.

Forgiveness reflects the very image of Jesus Christ. When Jesus was crucified on the cross for our sins, He wasn't crucified alone. Two criminals were executed with Him. The Bible tells us,

> Two others, both criminals, were led out to be executed with Him. When they came to a place called The Skull, they nailed Him to the cross. And the criminals were also crucified—one on His right and one on His left.
>
> Jesus said, "Father, forgive them, for they don't know what they are doing." And the soldiers gambled for His clothes by throwing dice. (Luke 23:32–34 (NLT))

Jesus asked the Father to forgive what seems to be unforgivable—the crucifixion of His only begotten Son. When we forgive, we reflect Jesus.

## 3 Forgiveness breaks down strongholds.

Forgiveness breaks down strongholds in our lives. When you forgive, you experience healing in your hurting heart. Forgiveness is the one major antidote to bitterness. Obedience to forgive brings freedom and enables you to start over in a relationship by the grace and mercy of God.

You can read about an example of restoration in the life of Joseph. His brothers had sold him into slavery out of jealousy (Genesis 37). Later, their positions of power were reversed.

Joseph was the second in command in Egypt with control over the food supply during a drought, and his brothers came to him for food (Genesis 41:39–42:7). Joseph could have been bitter over what they had done to him. But he wasn't. He forgave and helped them (Genesis 45:3–15). And because his brothers were repentant, Joseph's forgiveness paved the way for restoration in their relationship. Forgiveness brings freedom.

4 **Forgiveness relieves the offender's guilt.**
Forgiveness loosens the stranglehold of guilt in the offender. That person no longer has to rehearse their sin and carry it unforgiven by someone else. They actually become released by love and kindness.

As the Bible tells us,

> So God can point to us in all future ages as examples of the incredible wealth of His grace and kindness toward us, as shown in all He has done for us who are united with Christ Jesus. (Ephesians 2:7 (NLT))

God always points us to the wealth and favor of His kindness toward us. Forgiveness brings freedom to everyone involved.

Remember, we forgive because God has forgiven us in Christ. We didn't deserve to be forgiven. Nor did we earn that forgiveness. In turn, we must forgive others even if they don't deserve it. When we forgive, it relieves the oppressive burden of guilt. If Jesus had not extended kindness and forgiveness to sinners, we would forever exist in the stranglehold of guilt, sin, and darkness.

Let me remind you that forgiveness and reconciliation are two distinct things. Often, the confusion that comes with forgiveness is from confusing those two as one.

Forgiveness is an act of obedience in which you release a

debt. You acknowledge that someone hurt you. And then you make a conscious decision to release it and let it go.

You can forgive someone even if you can't tell them. Sometimes the unforgiveness in your life is tied to someone who has already passed away. Whether the person is available or not, you can release that person daily before the Lord when feelings of bitterness show up in your heart.

On the other hand, reconciliation is usually the natural by-product of forgiveness. But it requires an additional step by the other person. That additional step is repentance. Without repentance, there can be no restoration of the relationship. That's why it can be frustrating.

You may be thinking, *I've forgiven them, but nothing has changed.* But it's not entirely true that nothing has changed. By extending forgiveness, you're free. That's a huge thing. Don't discount the fact that you're free. And if the other person hasn't repented, keep forgiving any new wrongs while you're praying for repentance.

It's very powerful. And it's something that's good to revisit from time to time because there's always a new year, there are always new hurts, and there are always new difficulties and thoughts. The enemy is relentless.

But forgiveness is essential. It's a command. It's something that you're able to extend. And when you do, you will be free.

### *A Picture of Forgiveness*

Let's look at a beautiful picture of forgiveness from the life of King Jehoiachin. At the time, Jerusalem had fallen and the Babylonians put King Jehoiachin—the second to the last of the kings of Judah—in prison. King Jehoiachin had been in prison for 37 years.

During those 37 years, the king of Babylon, King Nebuchadnezzar, pridefully talked about *his* great power and *his* great possessions, only to be humbled by God. King Nebuchadnezzar declared, "Is not this great Babylon, that I have built for a royal dwelling by my mighty power and for the honor of my majesty?" (Daniel 4:30).

While the words were still in King Nebuchadnezzar's mouth, God gave him a mind of a beast. Imagine, the king of the known world—who had just conquered Judah and taken all of its possessions and people captive—was now like a beast. And he remained like that for seven years.

His son, Evil-Merodach, took his place to rule Babylon. Then, at the end of his seven years of madness, Nebuchadnezzar ended up praising God, returned to the throne, discovered the evil of his son's rule, and threw his son into prison.

But then Nebuchadnezzar died. And his son got out of prison and had the chance to rule again. So, let's look at what happened when Evil-Merodach got another chance.

> Now it came to pass in the thirty-seventh year of the captivity of Jehoiachin king of Judah, in the twelfth month, on the twenty-fifth day of the month, that Evil-Merodach king of Babylon, in the first year of his reign, lifted up the head of Jehoiachin king of Judah and brought him out of prison. And he spoke kindly to him and gave him a more prominent seat than those of the kings who were with him in Babylon. So Jehoiachin changed from his prison garments, and he ate bread regularly before the king all the days of his life. And as for his provisions, there was a regular ration given him by the king of Babylon, a portion for each day until the day of his death, all the days of his life. (Jeremiah 52:31–34)

One of the first things that Nebuchadnezzar's son did was to go to the prison and bring out Jehoiachin. He gave him a kingship higher than all the ones of the Babylonian kingdom. Imagine that. It's hard to think about being imprisoned for

37 years. It must have been a weird feeling, being released after all that time. I'm sure it was a very awkward adjustment. He had once been the king of Judah, had spent 37 years in confinement, and then, in an instant, he was free.

Over the years, I've found that many people get used to their captivity. They get used to where they are—to their sinful habits, the patterns of their flesh. Many have made unforgiveness their best friend. They've become friends with bitterness. They have more conversations with themselves about the people they're upset with than true prayer time with the Lord. People get used to their captivity. They become accustomed to being defined by their failures instead of by the power of God.

Sadly, some people would rather stay in their captivity than move into the freedom that the Lord gives through His grace and mercy. Remaining in captivity is not the will of Jesus Christ for you. He wants to set you free. In a very real way, we are set free as we take the steps of forgiveness. There's newness and forgiveness in Jesus.

*Remaining in captivity is not the will of Jesus Christ for you. He wants to set you free.*

It's a choice. In response to the forgiveness extended by Jesus, you can forgive. Or you can live in the shadow of your own condemnation. Because the anger and frustration that result from unforgiveness lead to regret—which often leads to condemnation—it will stifle the very life of Jesus Christ out of us.

You need to forgive yourself, and you need to forgive others. I know it's a painful process. God's forgiveness and your forgiveness don't eliminate the consequences of sin. Consequences come from our failures. And they come from other people's sinful actions. Those consequences remind us of what we did or what happened. It's very difficult.

Sometimes, God is very gracious and minimizes the consequences. Yet, other times we feel their full weight. And then if somebody responds sinfully, you also have to deal with that. It's painful.

But the place of abiding in Jesus—of resting in Him, receiving His forgiveness, and forgiving others—is the place of freedom. Like Jehoiachin, you may have a hard time not living in captivity. You may find it difficult to live in the newness of life.

If we can't forgive or receive forgiveness, we can't move on. We can't go forward. In unforgiveness, we're stuck. Unforgiveness equates to a prison of misery. Unforgiveness is often the reason we're not making progress in our relationship with God.

So, in Jeremiah 52, we observe the king of Babylon. He's not even a believer. He doesn't even love God. Yet, he shows more forgiveness than most give to others.

There are six things that we discover about forgiveness from the king releasing King Jehoiachin. And we learn of a greater King. We learn about the King of kings. He is greater than this king from Babylon. The King of kings descended into our prison of desperation and darkness. When we were lost and without any hope, wandering around blinded to our own sins, the King of kings died on the cross for those sins, so we could be forgiven. So, let's look at those six things.

# 1 Jehoiachin was brought out.

The king was the one who brought Jehoiachin out of prison. The Bible says, "Evil-Merodach king of Babylon, in the first year of his reign, lifted up the head of Jehoiachin king of Judah and brought him out of prison" (Jeremiah 52:31).

He brought him out. The king didn't send a messenger. He didn't send a servant. And he didn't have the prison guard release him. He chose to do it himself.

That's interesting to me. The king had been in captivity himself.

He was elevated to the throne after his dad died. For all intents and purposes, he was *the* leader of the known world at the time. And he took it upon himself to go back down into the very prison that he had just been released from to release King Jehoiachin.

And that's what God has done for us. The Creator of the universe Himself has forgiven us and set us free. He didn't send a messenger. He didn't send an angel. He didn't send a pastor or a priest. God Himself came down and delivered you from your prison of sin and darkness. God is ready to forgive all the rotten things we've ever done. All our sins have been buried, washed away, blotted out, and forgiven by Jesus Christ. He came Himself.

Jesus set aside His divine prerogatives and came to release us from our sins. And, "if the Son sets you free, you are truly free" (John 8:36 (NLT)). It's a done deal. Nobody can second-guess it. The King has the authority. And He came and took care of it Himself. I love that.

## 2 Jehoiachin was comforted.

The king comforted Jehoiachin. It says that "he spoke kindly to him and gave him a more prominent seat" (Jeremiah 52:32).

You know, the Church of Jesus could use more kindness. Obviously, the world could. But in the Church, we could be kinder and gentler with one another. We could cut each other some slack, especially when we're first out of captivity.

The king showed him kindness. I'm sure that after 37 years of imprisonment, Jehoiachin was discouraged, depressed, and hopeless. He likely had resigned himself to life in prison. But the king of Babylon encouraged him and gave him hope.

In the same way, God comes to us personally, lifts up our heads, and gives us hope. We're forgiven. And we're set free. But we might not have enough confidence. Or we may be in a weakened state.

Yet, we're surrounded by people who are running this race with us. You may not be in the lead, but you're surrounded by so many people. There's a guy who overcame this, and a gal who overcame that. The church is filled with overcomers. It shouldn't be a church filled with hypercritical judgment and finger-pointing. It should be filled with freedom.

Oh, it's not that we don't speak about the difficulties. It's not that we don't confront sin. Of course, we do. Kindly. And gently.

In Galatians 6, we see a New Testament illustration of what's happening here as the king has his head lifted. And I pray that you would take this to heart and become better at it. It says,

> Brethren, if a man is overtaken in any trespass, you who are spiritual restore such a one in a spirit of gentleness, considering yourself lest you also be tempted. Bear one another's burdens, and so fulfill the law of Christ. (Galatians 6:1–2)

Doesn't a heavy burden become half as heavy when someone helps you? Your burden is lightened when someone comes along to help you carry the load. The Bible says to bear one another's burdens, "For if anyone thinks himself to be something,"—that's where pride comes in—"when he is nothing,"—this is where humility comes in—"he deceives himself. But let each one examine his own work, and then he will have rejoicing in himself alone, and not in another. For each one shall bear his own load" (Galatians 6:3–5).

This is a gauge that shows where you're at spiritually. We all like to say we're spiritual. Do you want to know if you're spiritual? Look at how you respond when you see someone overtaken by a trespass. Because if you're spiritual, you'll want to rush in and restore him.

The word restore is actually a Greek word from the medical

community that speaks of putting together a broken bone.[3] When a bone is fractured, you reset that bone. And I've heard it said that once a bone is set after a break, it never breaks in the same place again. Perhaps it does in an exception. But it becomes stronger.

Imagine that. In our lives, the worst time can become the best time in the hands of the Lord. It takes some time for sure. In our worst place, we can't conceive how God could bring anything good out of it. But He does.

God restores and rebuilds. He helps us. And God lifts up our heads. He gives us hope as we're forgiven and set free. As it says in Psalm 3, "But You, O LORD, are a shield for me, my glory and the One who lifts up my head. I cried to the LORD with my voice, and He heard me from His holy hill" (Psalm 3:3–4). There's no longer a reason to hang our heads and condemn ourselves because we have freedom.

Never underestimate the power of a kind word, an encouraging text, a helpful note, a quick email, a phone call, or a knock on the door. Those are all ways you can show kindness, depending on your relationship with someone. But never underestimate the effect your kindness might have.

If you're driving to work one morning, listening to a song, and someone comes into your mind, act on it when you get to work.

Or maybe you're in your devotions, reading the Bible, and a Scripture pops out and sticks in your mind. You don't quite understand it because it doesn't really relate to anything in your life. But it really stuck out. It's like it jumped off the page. If you meditate on that Scripture, I assure you that God will bring a purpose to it.

And perhaps that purpose is someone you haven't seen at church in a while, a relative, or others who have crossed your path. Don't underestimate the power of kindness and encouragement.

I'm sure you've experienced the power of a kind word. You've also experienced the power of a word that wasn't fitly spoken. When we yield to God's Spirit, the kind word (rather than the misplaced one) will flow through us. The fruit of the Spirit is love, joy, peace, patience, kindness, goodness, faithfulness, gentleness, and self-control (Galatians 5:22–23).

The king didn't release Jehoiachin and then lay a heavy guilt trip on him. The king didn't ask him a series of accusing questions. He comforted him.

## 3 Jehoiachin was exalted.

The king exalted Jehoiachin. Not only did he speak kindly to him, he "gave him a more prominent seat than those of the kings who were with him in Babylon" (Jeremiah 52:32). The king restored Jehoiachin's life to what it had been before the enemy ripped him off.

And isn't that the work of God? God wants to restore what the enemy has stolen from you. He wants to bring you back and place your feet on a solid rock. He wants you to walk forward.

As the psalmist said, "my feet had almost stumbled; my steps had nearly slipped" (Psalm 73:2). The psalmist's statement means that it was almost over. *I was that close. I almost didn't come back.* And yet, he did come back. He came back stronger. It wasn't a series of slips. The psalmist writes it one time. And then he begins to extol the power of God to bring him off the ledge (Psalm 73:23–26).

We use that phrase from time to time, don't we? When someone's in a great crisis, we'll say something like, "We had the privilege of talking him off the ledge." And it really does speak of someone being at the end of his rope. There isn't anything more for him.

That's often the place of suicidal thoughts. It's a place of deep hopelessness. And whether it's real or imagined, it doesn't really matter. A person feels it either way. It's 100% real to him. We need to meet people where they're at. (If you are having suicidal thoughts even as you read this, please ask for help right away. Call a friend. Or call a hotline by dialing 988. There is help available right now.)

Some of the worst advice in a person's crisis is, "Oh, you shouldn't be feeling that. Why are you feeling that way?" Don't do that. Speak to people in their pain. Go down into the pit with them and escort them out. Remind them of God's power and the hope found in Him. Comfort them. Speak kindly. Lift up their heads. Point them toward Jesus so God can begin a work in their lives. Then their testimony will be: *My feet almost slipped. But God was faithful.*

Because we're just human, dealing with human things, we deal with our own sin. Even if we didn't deal with our own sin, we'd deal with everyone else's sin and the consequences of living in this painful world. The majority of the world lives in opposition to God. They hate God and have no morality about them. So, they're motivated only by their own greed and selfishness.

Are you overwhelmed by resentment and bitterness? Do you think your life is over—that it's impossible to rebound from a painful situation? I know many who have come down off the ledge. And we rejoice.

God has the power to bring you off the ledge. God forgives you, and He restores you. God's work in

> *God has the power to bring you off the ledge.*

your life will be overwhelming and breathtaking. Don't overlook the part of Psalm 23 where it tells you that your good Shepherd, Jesus, restores your soul (Psalm 23:3).

. . .

# 4 The king clothed Jehoiachin.

The king gave Jehoiachin new clothing. Not only was he brought out, comforted, and exalted, he was given new clothes. The Bible says, "So Jehoiachin changed from his prison garments" (Jeremiah 52:33). He was released from prison, encouraged, and given a throne. And then he put on a royal robe.

Jehoiachin had been in prison for 37 years. He was a king who was known as an enemy of Babylon. And what does he get? A royal robe.

Think about the great work that God does in our lives. He restores our nature. He restores our integrity. He restores our character. And He sees us in Christ. He sees us wearing the robes of righteousness. We don't come to Him with our own beggarly garments, trying to cover ourselves.

The Bible speaks of God taking away the garment of sadness and giving us the garment of praise. Jesus came,

> To console those who mourn in Zion, to give them beauty for ashes, the oil of joy for mourning, the garment of praise for the spirit of heaviness; that they may be called trees of righteousness, the planting of the LORD, that He may be glorified. (Isaiah 61:3)

Jesus shared a parable about a wedding, and a man didn't have the right garments. To be there, you needed to be given the right garments by the king (Matthew 22:11–12). As a follower of Jesus Christ, you are robed with the right garments. You're not wearing prison garments anymore. There are no longer shackles on your arms.

# 5 Jehoiachin was favored.

The king favored Jehoiachin. The Bible says, "he ate

bread regularly before the king all the days of his life" (Jeremiah 52:33). That basically means that he ate like a king. He ate like a king for the rest of his life. He no longer had to eat prison bread. Now, he had the bread of a king. It happened that fast. Instantly.

The king didn't abandon Jehoiachin. In fact, by his invitation to eat at his table, he wanted him to know that they would be friends forever.

When God forgives us, He draws us to Himself in relationship. Your relationship with God, by faith in Jesus Christ, is not a religious experience. The people on the stage don't do all the work for you. The pastor doesn't take care of everything you need.

Religion gives you the sense that you can never approach God. You're never good enough. You'll never make it. In religion, you work really hard, give a lot, go to the priest, and go through the motions. And *maybe* you'll make it to heaven. You'll find out after you die.

That's religion. Religion puts burdens on you. It places a barrier between you and God. That's not what God teaches us in His Word.

God comes to you personally. And He invites you to His table continually. You enjoy what the King enjoys. And He places you there. You don't take it upon yourself. You recognize the weak and beggarly condition of your life.

You'll never experience a relationship with Jesus Christ until you understand how far you are from Him. The Bible says that we've been separated from God by sin. There is no connection between man and God. We have all sinned and fallen short of God's glory, His perfection.

In other words, no one is perfect. We make allowances and excuses because none of us are perfect. But it's a serious condition to recognize. If you acknowledge that you're not perfect, you're saying, "I have sinned against you God. I have failed to live up to Your standard. I've failed to live the way You want me to live."

God is our Creator. He created us in His image. The purpose of our lives is to honor Him. And we're alive on the earth to make God known to those around us. That's why we're here. We once lived for ourselves, damaging our own and others' lives.

You know, we live in a culture that says, "Do whatever you want as long as it doesn't hurt anyone." Those who believe that philosophy forget that you can hurt yourself with your actions, disintegrating your soul.

An episode in my life comes to mind—one that happened before I started following Jesus. I remember going to jail and being violently beaten up in custody. I was injured enough that they called my dad to pick me up. They didn't tell him the extent of how bad my injuries really were.

You have to understand something about my dad. My dad is in the presence of the Lord now, but he wasn't a man of much emotion. He wasn't a man of much expression. He was a calm, quiet, and reliable guy. He loved his family. He was a faithful provider. My dad was not a man of great highs. And he definitely wasn't a man of great lows. We didn't see him get very angry. And we didn't see him incredibly happy.

I hardly ever recall seeing my dad cry. But when my dad picked me up from the police department, all bloodied and beaten up, he started weeping over the condition of his son. I remember it like it was yesterday.

You see, our decisions can hurt us. And they can hurt the people who love us. So, that philosophy isn't true. You can't do whatever you want because our poor decisions always end up hurting someone. We need to learn to think of others more than ourselves.

So, if you've come to the conclusion that you're not a perfect person, then you've hurt yourself and those who love you through your mistakes.

And there's only one remedy. The Bible says that the wages of sin—the wages of our mistakes—is always death (Romans 6:23). That death is all around us. The death of relationships. The death of hope. The death of strength. The death of marriages. Not just physical death, although physical death reminds us that sin is ever with us, but death in so many other areas where sin destroys.

Although the wages of sin is death, the gift of God is eternal life through Christ Jesus our Lord (Romans 6:23). The only remedy for where you're at right now is this: You talk to God, admit that you've failed Him, and receive His forgiveness. Yes, God the Creator, knowing everything about you, extends His forgiveness to you.

Jesus says, whoever will, let him come. You don't need to clean up your life first. God has made a way of escape for you. If you turn away from your sins, God will forgive you, right now while you're reading this. It doesn't really matter where you are. God is ready to forgive. The offer of salvation through Jesus Christ is available to all who will hear and come to Him.

Jesus says, if you believe, you'll be saved. If you don't believe, you'll be lost. It's really up to you. Forgiveness is available. And to enjoy forgiveness is to come to God and be honest. Tell Him about the condition of your life. And receive His forgiveness.

By receiving God's forgiveness, your life will be transformed. And one day, you'll be sitting at the table of the King of kings, enjoying the wedding feast of the Lamb (Revelation 19:9).

## 6 Jehoiachin's future was secure.

The king secured Jehoiachin's future. Forgiveness secures the future. Jehoiachin had nothing to worry about for the rest of his life. The king assured him that he would be taken care of all of his days. It says in Jeremiah 52:34, "as for his provisions, there was a regular ration given him by the king of Babylon, a portion for each day until the day of his death."

In Christ Jesus, you have an eternal hope that God will take care of you for the rest of your life. God has secured your future. And we've been given the promise of eternal life. *Nothing* can snatch you out of the Father's hands (John 10:29) or separate you from the love of God (Romans 8:39).

The greatest gift in our lives is God's forgiveness. Yet, it tends to be the most overlooked provision. We take it for granted. And by taking God's forgiveness for granted, we take our relationships for granted.

## The Need for True Forgiveness

Forgiveness that is not full is not true forgiveness. When a person says, "I'll forgive you, but I'll never forget"—that's not true, Biblical, loving forgiveness. It's kind of like saying, "Let's bury the hatchet," while leaving the handle showing so you can go get it any time you want.

*When God forgives us, it's a total, complete forgiveness.*

The problem with man is that our forgiveness isn't always true. Instead of forgiving like God does, we do it our own way. When we do that, we're putting ourselves in the place of God. We're basically saying, "If I was God, this is what I would do." And we neglect to put God on the throne where He belongs. He will not be dethroned. But you can live as if you're the one on the throne.

As I said, the problem with man is that our forgiveness isn't always true. We don't have a proper concept of forgiveness. We forget what true forgiveness is. We forget how God has forgiven us.

When God forgives us, it's a total, complete forgiveness. He promises to never remember our sin again (Hebrews 8:12 (quoting Jeremiah 31:34)). Our sin is separated from us as far as the east is from the west (Psalm 103:12). You will never have to answer to God for the sin that's been placed under the blood of Jesus Christ. It's gone. You have been washed. You are cleansed.

So, it's tragic that we say we forgive but then bring it up again and use it in our arguments. It's very prominent in marriages where one, or both, bring up the past. God wants you to forgive as He forgave you.

Now, you know as well as I do that the human mind is an amazing organ that God has created. And our memories are something really special. As much as we tend to forget, we remember a lot. When we speak of not remembering again, it really means that you choose not to hold it against the person.

There's a list we use in marriage discipleship called *Fight Rules*. One of those rules is: Don't use the past as a weapon.

God doesn't hold our past against us. We can't compare God's forgiveness with how we forgive one another because God's forgiveness is complete. You have been justified. It's more than being innocent or forgiven. It's being declared so innocent that it's as if you've never committed the sin to begin with.

God wipes the slate clean. He erases and blots out our transgressions. There's no need to look back. Press forward. God has forgiven it and wiped it away.

And we can ask God for His power to forgive. Remember, it's not something you can will yourself to do. That will lead to frustration and failure. But you can say, "I surrender myself to forgive," and ask God for His help to follow through.

It's "God who works in you both to will and to do for His good pleasure" (Philippians 2:13). It's God's work. It's His agape love—His true spiritual forgiveness. It comes from Him and through us.

And it's a beautiful thing to experience. Just like King Jehoiachin—37 years in captivity and, in an instant, he's changed. His life is one of the many pictures in the Bible of the great power of the blood of Jesus Christ.

# CHAPTER FIVE

## Dealing With Your Anger

I f you're going to walk in freedom from your past, you must deal with any lingering issues of sinful anger. There is a good anger. But there's also a bad anger.

The word anger in the New Testament actually comes from two Greek words. One means to have passion or energy. And the other means agitated or boiling.[1] So, there's a good anger and a bad anger.

Righteous anger is a God-given emotion that helps us solve problems. Examples of Biblical anger include David being upset over the injustice that Nathan the prophet shared with him (2 Samuel 12:5–6). And, of course, Jesus gave us an example of righteous anger when He went into the temple and flipped over the tables because they had defiled His Father's house (John 2:13–16).

When you think of righteous anger, notice that neither of these examples involved self-defense. Instead, they involved the defense of others or a Biblical principle.

Let's be clear that the anger I'm referring to in this chapter is sinful anger. Sinful anger is an outburst of wrath that the Bible calls a work of the flesh (Galatians 5:20). It's a sin.

There is an anger that God uses in our lives to move us to action. That anger arises from seeing unfairness or injustice. It warns us to avoid harm in the future.

But sinful, unrighteous anger is something that we need to deal with. And it needs to be dealt with quickly. Although it's sinful, it has been the most justified, excused sin within the Church.

More than 50% of people who go to a counselor or psychologist want help dealing with an anger issue in their lives.[2] That includes both believers and unbelievers. In my personal experience in ministering to people, that number is actually higher. So, the root of some things happening in your life—like divisions, marital issues, and parenting issues—is your unrighteous anger. And those issues can't be resolved unless you're willing to admit your anger is sinful and repent from it.

Anger arises when you're offended by something. It takes hold of you when you feel like something's outside of your control. When you feel that way, you try to manipulate the situation through anger.

It starts with the feeling that you've been wronged or that something is wrong. So, it comes from a place of hurt. There are deep hurts that lead to anger. But generally, it's a simple offense that sets it off.

For example, let's say you're driving on the highway to work. You're singing a worship song to the Lord. You're meditating on the Bible study you heard last Sunday. You couldn't be more in tune with heaven. You're encouraged. In fact, you're so encouraged that you need to remember to keep your hands on the steering wheel because you're driving. You're in the Spirit, enjoying what God's doing in your life.

Then what happens? Somebody cuts you off. And you feel offended. You're hurt by it. But you don't even sense the hurt. You don't acknowledge the offense because anger comes that fast.

You become a different person, and various responses follow. Some people get so caught up in it that they follow the person, catch up to him, and yell at him through closed windows. That's not going to help anything. But people do that.

Yeah, believers do that. If that's you, you probably ask yourself after you calm down, *What was I doing?* Because you haven't learned that everything's going to be fine. It's not that big a deal. Instead, you've got a habit of hurt—when you're hurt, you want to give it right back.

The other driver did something wrong. But rather than wondering if he was in a hurry, you're upset and offended—as if it's your lane and your highway. This is a real issue.

When you're offended, if you don't deal with it Biblically, it'll get worse. When you're offended, you get upset—not necessarily angry, but upset. If you don't deal with

*When you're offended, if you don't deal with it Biblically, it'll get worse.*

being upset, you become frustrated. And then frustration turns into bitterness. And now, *everybody* on the road is a horrible driver. Now you're bitter, and you become unforgiving.

And you wonder, *How did I get like this?* Well, you never dealt with the original offense. You never took that offense to the Lord and trusted in His sovereignty in your life.

The way to get out of this cycle is forgiveness. Just forgive. Release them from the debt that they owe you. And you can move forward in your life.

But when you do this for years, you can see how rooted anger can be in your life. Anger is devastating. It rips apart relationships. It destroys unity. And it hurts many.

The good news is that Jesus will help you. He can replace your wrath with the fruit of the Spirit. And He wants to deliver you today. He wants you to be free from anger. He wants you to walk in the Spirit. If you're a born-again believer, He dwells in you. He will do a work in your life if you confess your sin and surrender your life to Him.

You know as well as I do—your angry self is not getting you what you want. I have met many people who regret the life of anger they've lived. It's kind of like God laying a whole feast out for you and saying, "Come and enjoy the feast. Look at the meal I provided for you." And you're eating a warmed-up Big Mac that you bought last week. And it has green things growing on it. God's given you everything to live an abundant life. And you're settling for so much less.

Nebuchadnezzar gives us an example of someone with an anger issue. In Daniel 2, it says,

> Now in the second year of Nebuchadnezzar's reign, Nebuchadnezzar had dreams; and his spirit was so troubled that his sleep left him. Then the king gave the command to call the magicians, the astrologers, the sorcerers, and the Chaldeans to tell the king his dreams. So they came and stood before the king. And the king said to them, "I have had a dream, and my spirit is anxious to know the dream."
>
> Then the Chaldeans spoke to the king in Aramaic, "O king, live forever! Tell your servants the dream, and we will give the interpretation."
>
> The king answered and said to the Chaldeans, "My decision is firm: if you do not make known the dream to me, and its interpretation, you shall be cut in pieces, and your houses shall be made an ash heap." (Daniel 2:1–5)

I think it's safe to say that Nebuchadnezzar had a serious issue with anger in his life. If things didn't go his way, he was ready to use his power to hurt someone. He literally threatened to kill them. And he had the power to do it. He threatened to burn down all of their houses, where their families lived. But it didn't stop there.

- A little later, the Bible tells us, "For this reason the king was angry and very furious, and gave the command to destroy all the wise men of Babylon" (Daniel 2:12).
- And in another instance, it says, "Then Nebuchadnezzar, in rage and fury, gave the command to bring Shadrach, Meshach, and Abed-Nego. So they brought these men before the king" (Daniel 3:13).
- And then, "Nebuchadnezzar was full of fury, and the expression on his face changed toward Shadrach, Meshach, and Abed-Nego" (Daniel 3:19).

Nebuchadnezzar's anger progressed, and he was filled with rage and fury.

Anger is destructive. Like a fire, it destroys everything in its path. It destroys people—the people whom Jesus died for, including the angry person. This emotion can be so destructive, so hurtful, that it will forever harm the person it's pointed toward.

And like I said, it's also an area in a believer's life that's often excused. You've probably heard someone say, "I'm this kind of ethnicity, so we're always angry." But that's just an excuse. Or maybe you've heard someone justify her anger by saying, "He deserved it!" Others claim it was righteous anger. Come on now. An outburst of wrath isn't righteous. God doesn't want us to justify our anger. He wants us to confess it and forsake it.

There are certain times when anger is appropriate. Yes, there can be righteous anger when you see sin and evil. But that's not King Nebuchadnezzar here. And that's not what we're talking about. Sinful anger is our target. And God forbids sinful anger and enables us with the power of His Spirit to avoid it.

God can deliver you from your anger. I would even put it this way: God *has* delivered you from your anger as a born-again believer in Jesus Christ. And you can walk in the freedom God's given you when you respond to Him by faith and trust Him to do the work. If you let Him, God will replace your anger with the fruit of His Spirit. Then, instead of anger, you'll be filled with love, joy, peace, patience, kindness, and goodness.

## *Worldly Wisdom about Anger*

You can get wisdom on the topic of anger from the world. Or you can get it from the Bible. In this chapter, we will look at Biblical wisdom on anger. But first, let's look at how the world views anger.

There are some great suggestions available to us in our world. Professionals will help you with some of the outward things. But worldly wisdom is not the same as God's wisdom. And that's an important distinction to make.

I came across an article from a very trusted medical community known as the Mayo Clinic—*Anger Management: 10 tips to tame your temper.*[3] Here's what the Mayo Clinic recommends.

1. Think before you speak

In the heat of the moment, it's easy to say something you'll later regret. Take a few moments to collect your thoughts before saying anything. Also allow others involved in the situation to do the same.

That may sound great at first. But if you've ever been in an anger episode, either someone else or yourself, it's already too late to collect your thoughts. You've already lost your ability to reason. You're out of control.

2. Once you're calm, express your concerns

As soon as you're thinking clearly, express your frustration in an assertive but nonconfrontational way. State your concerns and needs clearly and directly, without hurting others or trying to control them.

### 3. Get some exercise

Physical activity can help reduce stress that can cause you to become angry. If you feel your anger escalating, go for a brisk walk or run. Or spend some time doing other enjoyable physical activities.

How about that one? Get some exercise and sweat it out. Physical activity can reduce stress. I like to sweat things out.

### 4. Take a timeout

Timeouts aren't just for kids. Give yourself short breaks during times of the day that tend to be stressful. A few moments of quiet time might help you feel better prepared to handle what's ahead without getting irritated or angry.

Put yourself in a timeout. Timeouts are not just for kids. But in an angry episode, take a timeout? It's good to pause and take a breath.

### 5. Identify possible solutions

Instead of focusing on what made you mad, work on resolving the issue at hand. Does your child's messy room make you upset? Close the door. Is your partner late for dinner every night? Schedule meals later in the evening. Or agree to eat on your own a few times a week. Also, understand that some things are simply out of your control. Try to be realistic about what you can and cannot change. Remind yourself that anger won't fix anything and might only make it worse.

### 6. Stick with "I" statements

Criticizing or placing blame might only increase tension.

Instead, use "I" statements to describe the problem. Be respectful and specific. For example, say, "I'm upset that you left the table without offering to help with the dishes" instead of "You never do any housework."

Again, by the time you're in an anger episode, it's too late.

7. Don't hold a grudge

Forgiveness is a powerful tool. If you allow anger and other negative feelings to crowd out positive feelings, you might find yourself swallowed up by your own bitterness or sense of injustice. Forgiving someone who angered you might help you both learn from the situation and strengthen your relationship.

This one is very Biblical. Don't hold a grudge. They tap on very good wisdom there. Forgive and release.

8. Use humor to release tension

Lightening up can help diffuse tension. Use humor to help you face what's making you angry and, possibly, any unrealistic expectations you have for how things should go. Avoid sarcasm, though—it can hurt feelings and make things worse.

9. Practice relaxation skills

When your temper flares, put relaxation skills to work. Practice deep-breathing exercises, imagine a relaxing scene, or repeat a calming word or phrase, such as "Take it easy." You might also listen to music, write in a journal . . . —whatever it takes to encourage relaxation.

Can you imagine? "Take it easy." You're like, "I don't want to take it easy!" I'm not making it up. It says right here, "Take it easy."

10. Know when to seek help

Learning to control anger can be a challenge at times. Seek help for anger issues if your anger seems out of control, causes you to do things your regret or hurts those around you.

Seeking help is wise. So, don't be prideful about it. Ask for help.

Worldly wisdom has some good tips. I'm not minimizing tips. Do whatever it takes to bring down your temper a notch. Use tools—anything short of sin—so you're not flipping out all the time. I agree. But if you only listen to the way the world approaches the topic, you'll never deal with the root issue.

## *Biblical Wisdom about Anger*

The root issue of anger is very simple. You're a sinner. It's a rooted bitterness in your heart. Your attempt to control the situation by yelling, screaming, or whatever you're doing is a sin that needs to be confessed and repented of. That's the root.

The root issue is a spiritual one. It's an issue with your heart. And if you neglect the root issue, things won't improve. It's not by might and it's not by power, but it's "'by My Spirit,' says the LORD of hosts" (Zechariah 4:6). It's God's ability, not yours.

So, let me establish for you that there is such a thing as sinful anger. The Bible says,

Understand this, my dear brothers and sisters: You must all be quick to listen, slow to speak, and slow to get angry. Human anger does not produce the righteousness God desires. (James 1:19–20 (NLT))

Listen to the Bible. Your anger can never make things right in God's sight. Just accept that by faith. That's what God teaches us in His Bible. He's the One who created us. He knows us best.

**85**

Your anger can never make things right in God's sight. As the New King James Version puts it, "the wrath of man does not produce the righteousness of God" (James 1:20).

Never. Anger never makes anything right. This is an important principle to hold on to. The wrath of man is not going to take you where you want to go.

But in the Spirit—when you submit to Him—God can temper your temper. Jesus can strengthen you and teach you how to take it down a notch. You won't get there by repeating little words and phrases. Rather, Jesus will literally remove the root of anger from your heart and enable you to forgive.

As Proverbs 29:11 says, "A fool vents all his feelings, but a wise man holds them back." It's not okay to blow up. It's not okay.

A young lady once came to the great evangelist, Billy Sunday, after he delivered a strong, stirring message on the topic of anger. She was trying to rationalize, justify, and explain away her anger. So, she told the pastor after the service, "There's nothing wrong with losing my temper. I blow up, and then it's all over." To which the pastor replied, "So does a shotgun, and look at the damage that it leaves behind."[4]

It's true. Anger always leaves damage. And sometimes it leaves long-term damage.

Anger is a universal issue. It affects those who follow God and those who don't. We looked at an example of someone who wasn't following God—Nebuchadnezzar. Now, let's look at an example of someone who did.

You might be surprised by his name. His name is Moses. Moses had a serious anger issue. And it ruined his life. Moses didn't enter the promised land because of his anger.

Anger is a devastating emotion. And we see it throughout Moses's life. He never dealt with his anger, and it cost him greatly. Even mighty men of God can make serious mistakes.

I've seen it lived out today—where someone doesn't deal

with anger. You have an outburst, and you get on with life. Then you have another outburst, and you get on with life. And you might not think it's a big deal. After all, your family's still together. You haven't lost your job. But it is a big deal. Every single time.

Don't confuse God's patience with His approval. Don't confuse the mercy of people around you by concluding that they didn't get hurt by what you said or did. The email you sent was actually pretty nasty, and you shouldn't have sent it. You should've prayed. You know what you posted on Facebook because you had an opinion. The post actually hurt people and stumbled others. And it's possible that you're not aware of the consequences of your anger because you had been in such a rage that you don't remember.

You've got to deal with your anger. If you don't, you could miss out on the promises of God. Of course, you'll still be a believer. But you won't fully receive all that God has for you. You'll be stuck until you're willing to confess and forsake the sin of anger.

For Moses, it started in Exodus 2 when he killed a guy. He literally killed someone. He thought he was doing something good for God. When he saw a fight between a Hebrew and an Egyptian, he went over and killed the Egyptian. Because of it, he spent the next 40 years in the desert.

Did you know that murder is tied to anger? It is. Some Christians think they're okay because they've never murdered anyone. But you've got to listen to Jesus very carefully. When He started teaching about heart issues, Jesus said,

> You have heard that it was said to those of old, "You shall not murder, and whoever murders will be in danger of the judgment." But I say to you that whoever is angry with his brother without a cause shall be in danger of the judgment. (Matthew 5:21–22)

If you have anger in your heart toward someone, it's as if you've murdered them in your heart. We're more guilty of things than we're willing to admit. If we come to Jesus Christ and allow Him to teach us and lead us, He has freedom waiting for us.

After Moses was in the desert for 40 years, God brought him back. And Moses started obeying God. He got to see God. He got to hear from God. He led the children of Israel out of slavery. He stood up to Pharaoh. I mean, that's an amazing thing. God was doing a great work in Moses's life.

But then, we see his anger again. And his anger got the best of him. And it hurt him.

The Bible describes Moses as "very humble, more than all men who were on the face of the earth" (Numbers 12:3). Most of the time, he was faithful, sensitive, obedient, and self-sacrificial. But he also had an area inside himself that he never dealt with. There was an ongoing struggle throughout his life. So, Moses would sin in anger, and then he'd be obedient.

We see Moses's anger rise again in Exodus 16. He had given the Israelites God's instruction to only gather enough manna— that miraculous bread from heaven that God gave them to eat— for one day. Moses told them not to keep any of it until morning (Exodus 16:16–19).

> But some of them didn't listen and kept some of it until morning. But by then it was full of maggots and had a terrible smell. Moses was very angry with them. (Exodus 16:20 (NLT))

It says that Moses was *very angry* with them. And then he returned to a life of obedience.

But then we come to another episode of anger. This time, the Bible says that Moses "burned with anger" (Exodus 32:19 (NLT)). His anger was progressive. And it would be this last episode that would hold him back.

## *A Parent's Anger Is Destructive*

Before we get to that, I want to speak to parents who have anger issues. Please hear me. Sinful anger is destructive to your children. Some of you are self-deceived into thinking that your anger is raising righteous and godly kids who will love God with all their hearts, soul, and mind. It's not. It's actually doing the exact opposite. Your out-of-control anger is damaging your kids.

I understand that you may have been raised by an angry parent or grandparent. So, maybe you think that's just how it is. That's how your grandfather was, that's how your dad was, and that's just how you are. They were okay, and I'll be okay too.

But if you carefully examine your dad and your grandpa, you'd find that they didn't make it out as okay as you think. Their parents' anger deeply wounded them. And hurt them. That's why they became angry. And the anger then was handed down from each person, mom or dad.

I know from experience. I grew up in a very angry home. My parents were very loving and wonderful. But one of my parents chose to parent in an angry way. I'll admit that I was a challenging and difficult kid. But challenging and difficult kids don't deserve angry parents.

I assure you that I'm okay now. We settled everything a long time ago, and there's been forgiveness. They did the best they could with what they had. God was gracious and merciful to us. And all is well. They're in heaven right now rejoicing.

Although it's not unusual to have an anger streak because of how you were raised, I don't want you to be self-deceived anymore. I want you to understand what happens when you run your house with anger. There are four things that happen when your kids live in an angry home.

. . .

1 **You get compliance.**
When you're angry and out of control with your kids, you're going to get compliance. They will do what you tell them to do. But don't confuse their compliance with godly obedience. That's not what it is. Generally, it's not godly obedience. Your kids aren't necessarily complying with the Lord.

Instead, they're scared. And they want you to stop. They're smart enough to know what's going on. They're scared, and they will do whatever it takes for you to stop and calm down.

2 **Your kids begin to harden their hearts.**
When you're angry with your kids, the second thing that happens is they begin to harden their hearts. They're actually hardening their hearts toward you. It's very difficult to follow an angry person. Anger breaks the line of trust. It's hard to trust someone that you're scared of.

And your kids aren't going to tell you because they're afraid of you. And when children are small, they don't understand. They're just developing their thinking. They don't know how to deduce that something is massively wrong in their house. They don't know how to talk to their parents about it. They're just kids.

3 **Your kids become fearful.**
The third thing that happens in an angry home is your kids become fearful. Although this is part of the second point, I want you to understand the size difference between you and your kids.

I'm six foot one. If your kiddos come up to hug me and they're two and a half feet tall, I'm a monster to them. I'm huge.

We don't look at things from that perspective anymore. But your kiddos are small, and I'm tall.

And you're bigger than your kids. You're stronger than they are. You're more capable of doing things. So, when you fly off the handle, they're scared. And they shut down and harden their hearts toward you. You think they're obeying, but they're just scared.

# 4 Your kids learn to avoid you.

The fourth thing that happens with your kids is something I call avoidance. We all want the same thing with our kids. We want them to love God and serve Him with all their hearts, soul, and mind. And we want to enjoy our kids all the way to eternity. We want them to be a part of our lives.

But if they grow up in an angry home, they learn to avoid you at a young age. The less time they have to face your anger, the better. So, they choose to avoid you. And if that never gets corrected, they continue to avoid you as adults. They just don't want to deal with it.

Then, if you mix in drugs, alcohol, and drunkenness, it's a disaster. And yes, I'm still talking about Christian homes. In the homes of those who say they follow God.

If you didn't know these things, God wants to reveal them to you. Your kids are precious in the sight of the Lord. And I know that you love them. And it's never too late to get back on track. You can still express love to your kids.

Before I was saved, anger was a predominant thing in my life. And that's partly because it was the kind of home I grew up in. But it was also because I chose to. It was my responsibility. As I grew older, I entered into a serious relationship with my wife and that's how I treated her. And when we had our son, that's how I treated him. I started raising my son by yelling at him. My home was an angry home.

But then I got saved. I was born again. And God delivered me from that root of anger. God began that sanctifying work in me. God replaced that thinking with the right kind of thinking. God taught me to love my kids and serve them. I learned to encourage them, disciple them, and train them.

Now, no parent is perfect. Don't expect perfection from yourself. God meets us where we're at in His grace. But I'm going to give you a tool that will stop the madness. God gave it to me. And it will do a work in you and your kids. Of all the tools God gave me as a parent, this has been, by far, the most important one. It's been one of the most effective. It's something I never saw or heard growing up.

I want you to learn how to get down on your knees where you're at eye level with your kids. Then look your kids in the eye and say, "Will you forgive me? I was wrong, and I sinned against you in my anger." And ask your kids, "Will you pray for me?"

I'm telling you, it's one of the most powerful, God-honoring things that you can do in your life. And it's never too late.

Those little kiddos grow up. But you can still do this. It opens the floodgates, which leads to forgiveness. It opens the door for God to do a work of reconciliation between you and your kids. And you'll be free.

There are a lot of studies that show how the Church is losing kids after high school. Once those kids grow up, they're not walking with God anymore. I'm going to suggest to you that kids who lived in angry homes stopped walking with God in the third grade. They went to Sunday school and learned something about God. And then, boom, they were right back into homes filled with anger.

It's devastating. I know there are a lot of reasons why kids aren't following the Lord later on. But some of them didn't live in a home that honored God. In their home, anger was the predominant emotion. And now, they equate God with anger. God wants to release you.

### The Last Episode of Anger in Moses's Life

We see the last episode of anger in Moses's life in Numbers 20. After the other episodes, God was gracious. But in the last one, Moses went too far.

And the last one in your life will be you going too far. I promise you. Most of the time, the reason people come in to speak with a pastor is because of their last time of anger. It's the last episode of your anger when . . .

- *you find yourself in the back of a police car.*
- *you end up getting drunk in a bar and hurting someone.*
- *your wife finally walks out on you and files the papers.*
- *your kids rebel.*

But it doesn't have to happen like that.

You see, the last episode of your anger could be met with repentance. You don't have to go that far. And I'm not talking about times when you get frustrated. We all get frustrated sometimes. I'm talking about the ongoing outbursts of wrath and sinful anger that surround your life. And the last one, you'll regret—unless you repent before you go that far.

Let's see what happened with Moses.

Then the LORD spoke to Moses, saying, "Take the rod; you and your brother Aaron gather the congregation together. Speak to the rock before their eyes." (Numbers 20:7–8)

God told Moses to speak to the rock. How do we speak? With our mouths. It's very simple. If you were Moses, would you understand what to do? Speak to the rock. Pretty easy.

Imagine that you're sitting at your kitchen table in the morning, doing your devos. And God tells you, "Go out into your backyard and speak to the rock." You would know what He's telling you to do. I know it's elementary. But sometimes we need to make it super simple. Otherwise, we take what God's Word says and twist it. And that's when we get in trouble.

So, God told Moses to speak to the rock. And then God told Moses what would happen. God said,

> it will yield its water; thus you shall bring water for them out of
> the rock, and give drink to the congregation and their animals.
> (Numbers 20:8)

We learn something about God here. He wants to quench the thirst of the children of Israel. That's what He wants to do. He wants to bless them. He wants to take care of them. And He wants to use Moses to do it, so they'll get the water they need for themselves and their animals. God loves them.

Now, Moses has dealt with years of rebellion from the people. He's had years of difficulty as he led them. Yet, what's God's perspective? "I love them. Give them the water. And Moses, this is how you're going to do it. It's going to be a great miracle. Go to the rock, talk to it, and everybody's going to be happy."

All right Moses. What did you do?

> So Moses took the rod from before the LORD as He commanded
> him. And Moses and Aaron gathered the assembly together
> before the rock; and he said to *them* . . . . (Numbers 20:9–10
> (emphasis added))

Whoa, wait a minute. What did God say? Speak to the rock. What did Moses do? He spoke to them.

I'm sure you've made that mistake before. God makes something so clear to you. And on the way, you change it.

Why did Moses change it? Because he was angry. The truth of God gets distorted when we live in the flesh. Moses is an angry man. And instead of speaking to the rock, he speaks to them. And Moses said,

Hear now, you rebels! Must we bring water for you out of this rock? (Numbers 20:10)

And it doesn't end there. It gets worse. Moses took his rod, and he struck the rock. The Bible tells us,

Then Moses lifted his hand and struck the rock twice with his rod; and water came out abundantly, and the congregation and their animals drank. (Numbers 20:11)

Moses did the wrong thing more than one time. He expressed anger. Then he hit the rock and water came out.

Do you know the conclusion he might have come to? And maybe you would come to the same conclusion. He might have decided that he did it the right way because water came out. Maybe he thought, *Oh, I know God told me to speak to the rock. I did it my way. But water came out. So, it's okay. Everything's fine. I got what I wanted. The people got what they wanted.*

But that's not how God views our disobedience. Our disobedience is just that in the eyes of God. It's sinful. When God tells you to speak to the rock, speak to it. And don't strike it at all.

And notice what Moses didn't know. A lot of the time, God will tell you to do something. And you don't know why. God may be working in your life right now. But you don't know why the situation's in your life. You don't know why He gave you a certain instruction. You don't know. But the fact that we don't know is no excuse to be disobedient.

Moses didn't know that the rock was a picture and a type of Jesus Christ. In the New Testament, it tells us,

> For they drank of that spiritual Rock that followed them, and
> that Rock was Christ. (1 Corinthians 10:4)

God used that rock in giving forth water as a picture. Later,
Jesus would stand on the teaching steps going into the Temple.
And He would say,

> If anyone thirsts, let him come to Me and drink. He who
> believes in Me, as the Scripture has said, out of his heart will
> flow rivers of living water. (John 7:37–38)

The rock was a picture of Jesus. And when Jesus was struck,
he was struck once, not twice.

So, you can get clear direction from God and totally mess it
up. God will still accomplish what He wants to do. But don't
think God is pleased by your disobedience. Just because God still
did what He said He would do, it doesn't mean He's pleased with
you doing it your own way.

And God wasn't pleased with Moses either. The Bible says,
"Then the LORD spoke to Moses and Aaron, 'Because you did
not believe Me . . . .'" (Numbers 20:12).

Pause there for a second. Where in the text does it say that
Moses didn't believe God? It doesn't. God looked at Moses's life
and said, "Your anger made you an unbeliever." Anger is a form
of unbelief.

So, God told Moses and Aaron,

> Because you didn't believe Me, to hallow Me in the eyes of the
> children of Israel, therefore you shall not bring this assembly
> into the land which I have given them. (Numbers 20:12)

Now, many times, I've been taught that Moses didn't honor
the Lord. That's true. And now you understand *why* he didn't
represent God properly. It was his anger and his disobedience.

Moses twisted the Word of God. He didn't completely obey. God loved those people even in their rebellion, just like He loves you. That's why Moses didn't enter the promised land.

## *The Five Essentials of Righteous Anger*

If you still think your anger is okay, here are five things you should ask yourself when you start to justify your anger. If *all* five are present at the same time, then it's okay to be angry.

1. You're angry, and you don't sin (Ephesians 4:26).

2. You're angry, and you don't go to sleep with it. You don't let "the sun go down on your wrath" (Ephesians 4:26).

3. Your anger is from God—not from your own selfishness and desire to control, which are works of the flesh (Galatians 5:19–20).

4. Your anger achieves the righteousness of God "for the wrath of man does not produce the righteousness of God" (James 1:20).

5. Your anger comes slowly (Proverbs 16:32).

If you have all five of those things, then you can proceed carefully and safely with anger. Rarely do those things occur at the same time in our lives. Anger is usually a control mechanism. A lot of our anger comes from annoyances. And anger, unforgiveness, and bitterness are all cousins.

## *Sinful Anger Is a Heart Issue*

Sinful anger is not from the Lord for any of us. As the Bible tells us, *now* is the time to get rid of anger (Colossians 3:8). And "[a]n angry person starts fights" (Proverbs 29:22 (NLT)).

Anger is a heart issue. As Jesus said,

> A good tree can't produce bad fruit, and a bad tree can't produce good fruit. A tree is identified by its fruit. Figs are never gathered from thornbushes, and grapes are not picked from bramble bushes. A good person produces good things from the treasury of a good heart, and an evil person produces evil things from the treasury of an evil heart. *What you say flows from what is in your heart.* (Luke 6:43–45 (NLT) (emphasis added))

Or as the New King James Version phrases that last part, "For out of the abundance of the heart his mouth speaks" (Luke 6:45).

So, Jesus teaches us that anger is a heart issue. That's it. The problem with your anger is a heart issue. And because we don't know our own hearts, the Bible tells us to ask God to reveal what's in them. Like the psalmist, you can say,

> Search me, O God, and know my heart; test me and know my anxious thoughts. Point out anything in me that offends you, and lead me along the path of everlasting life. (Psalm 139:23 (NLT))

Ask God to reveal any hidden sin in you. Ask Him to show you what offends you and hurts others. After He reveals it, follow what 1 John 1:9 tells you to do, "If we confess our sins, He is faithful and just to forgive us our sins and to cleanse us from all unrighteousness."

Don't just feel bad about your anger. Confess it. Repent of it as the sin that it is. And let God start to do the work in your heart.

As you let God do the work in your heart, start filling your heart and mind with the things the Bible tells us to think about. Fix your thoughts on things that are true, noble, just, pure, lovely, and of good report. Think about things that are virtuous and praiseworthy (Philippians 4:8).

If you meditate on good things, the abundance of your heart will be filled with the grace of God and His mercy. He'll give you that grace and mercy because He loves you. And while you're still alive, it's never too late to get right with God.

Moses didn't ever get into the promised land. Or did he? A careful reading of the Scriptures tells us that he didn't get in with that generation. He died on the other side of the promised land (Deuteronomy 34:1–5).

But by God's grace, he did get into the promised land. That's how much God loved Moses. Remember when Jesus was up on

*God forbids sin in our lives because it destroys us.*

the Mount of Transfiguration? While He was there, He was met by two people who are fully alive (Matthew 17:1–3). Their names? Elijah and Moses. You bet he got in.

God loves you too. He's gracious, caring, and compassionate. And He wants what's best for you and your family. God doesn't forbid sin just because it's against His holiness and His glory, although that is a serious thing. God forbids sin in our lives because it destroys us. And any good dad wants to protect his kids from things that will destroy them.

I'm a living example that God can change someone's life. Before my son passed away, we settled all the stuff that happened when he was a little guy. He was so forgiving and loving. And then my other children were born into a godly home. They weren't born to perfect parents. But they were born to growing, sanctifying parents—ones who worked out their differences, humbled themselves, asked each other for forgiveness, and let the Spirit of God work through their weaknesses.

That's God's will for your family too. It's His will for your kids, your grandkids, and your marriage. He wants to work in your family by His Spirit.

For those who still aren't convinced that anger is a big deal, here are just a few verses from the Proverbs and Psalms that talk about anger:

- "A fool is quick-tempered, but a wise person stays calm when insulted" (Proverbs 12:16 (NLT)).
- "Short-tempered people do foolish things, and schemers are hated" (Proverbs 14:17 (NLT)).
- "People with understanding control their anger; a hot temper shows great foolishness" (Proverbs 14:29 (NLT)).
- "A hot-tempered person starts fights; a cool-tempered person stops them" (Proverbs 15:18 (NLT)).
- "Better to be patient than powerful; better to have self-control than to conquer a city" (Proverbs 16:32 (NLT)).
- "Sensible people control their temper; they earn respect by over-looking wrongs" (Proverbs 19:11 (NLT)).
- "Fools vent their anger, but the wise quietly hold it back" (Proverbs 29:11 (NLT)).
- "Stop being angry! Turn from your rage! Do not lose your temper—it only leads to harm" (Psalm 37:8 (NLT)).

The Bible has a lot to say about sinful anger. Sinful anger hurts others. And it hurts you.

A Bible study like this requires a response. If you have a problem with anger, you need to confess that sin. Pray to God and admit that you have a problem with anger. Agree with God that it's a sin. Tell God you want to do things His way now. Cry it out. Let God wash you with the tears you shed. Every single tear you shed is kept in a bottle by God (Psalm 56:8). Allow God to cleanse you.

You can't change the past. But you can change the future. And that's God's will for you. He wants you to be alive and filled with His Spirit. He doesn't want you hiding sin. And He doesn't want you to be a victim of abuse or the one giving abuse. He wants cleanliness and purity. And He's doing the work. You just need to meet Him there.

# CHAPTER
# SIX

## Dealing With The Present

B y this point, you've learned many Biblical truths that will
help you to get free from your past. But now, I want to
show you where you get the power to put those Biblical truths
into practice. You'll find that power day by day and moment by
moment in Jesus. You need to abide in Him.

In John 15, God gives us a beautiful picture of the vine and
the vinedresser. Jesus said,

> I am the true vine, and My Father is the vinedresser. Every
> branch in Me that does not bear fruit He takes away; and every
> branch that bears fruit He prunes, that it may bear more fruit.
> You are already clean because of the word which I have spoken
> to you. Abide in Me, and I in you. As the branch cannot bear
> fruit of itself, unless it abides in the vine, neither can you,
> unless you abide in Me.
>
> I am the vine, you are the branches. He who abides in Me,
> and I in him, bears much fruit; for without Me you can do
> nothing. (John 15:1–5)

In this passage, Jesus brings us back to what's very important in our relationship with Him. It's not religious expression. It is not our religious heritage. It's not the activities that we do. The thing we need to learn how to do in our relationship with Him is to abide.

Relationship paints a beautiful picture. We all have relationships at the human level. We know that relationships grow over time. They grow with time and testing. It's not a formality.

If following Jesus was just a bunch of outward activities, many Christians would be very good followers because we know how to do things outwardly. But it's not about the outward. It's about the inward.

In these verses, we learn just how well the vinedresser takes care of us. That's the emphasis. The vinedresser cultivates the vineyard and tends the vine. The vinedresser is a picture of God the Father, the true vine is a picture of Jesus, and the branches are a picture of born-again believers.

God the Father, as the vinedresser, is the One who cares for us. And as born-again believers, we need to be connected to the true vine, Jesus, if we want to grow and be fruitful. We receive all of our spiritual nourishment through our connection to Him.

I know there are many who love to garden. When spring comes, it's gardening time. Gardeners care for the plants they grow in a wonderful way. They study. They determine the right soil, light, and all that goes into it.

Imagine how much more the Father cares for you. Think about how much He takes care of you. And like He did with the nation of Israel, God is still looking for fruit among His Church.

The good news is that our fruit—like the fruit on a tree or the grapes on a vine—occurs naturally. It occurs through our relationship with God.

Most of us don't think too much about it. And some of us

don't care. But when you see fruit or a flower, remember that happens through relationship.

There's no need for a tree to work hard to try to produce fruit. You don't hear groaning as you walk by a tree. Trees aren't making faces. They're not stressing out because they need to produce fruit. That's not how it works. Instead, when a tree is planted by the right farmer in the right area and is given water and the right nutrients, it grows and fruit comes naturally.

You may wonder why I'm telling you about fruit. The truth is that you're in your best place as a believer as you abide in Christ and produce fruit. Think of it this way: the production of fruit in your life is the natural outcome of God's presence in your life. So, if there's no fruit from your life, it shows that you're not abiding.

And when you're not abiding, the Bible calls that being in your flesh. In your flesh, you rely on your own resources, which are all empty. You won't have the power you need to move forward from your past if you're not abiding.

The Bible tells us about the fruit that is produced in your life as a result of abiding in Jesus. This fruit will occur naturally in your life as you abide in Him:

- Winning souls (Romans 1:13).
- Holiness (Romans 6:22).
- Giving financially (Romans 15:28).
- Helping others practically (Colossians 1:6).
- Giving praise to God (Hebrews 13:15).
- Love (Galatians 5:22).

There are other fruit of the Spirit listed in Galatians. Many believe they are all a manifestation of one fruit of the Spirit— love. Others look at them separately. I think it could go either way. In addition to love, the fruit of the Spirit is joy, peace, patience, kindness, goodness, faithfulness, gentleness, and self-control (Galatians 5:22–23).

The key to bearing fruit is given to us in John 15. It's the word abide. Why is abiding so important? Abiding is necessary because Jesus tells us, "without Me, you can do nothing" (John 15:5).

It's very important for us to fully understand that truth. As we walk with Jesus Christ and serve Him, we can't do anything without Him. As I exercise the gift of pastor-teacher and as I have the privilege of leading and serving, I must remember— without Jesus, I can do nothing.

Sure, we can do a lot of things without Jesus. We can produce things. We can engage in religious activities. We can be very active and busy. We can even do things in Jesus' name, without Jesus. But I'm telling you this—without Jesus, you can do nothing of eternal value. You can't do anything that reflects His love and His character.

But Jesus can take a person from having no fruit to producing much fruit by His indwelling presence. The key is abiding. It's the difference between walking in the flesh and walking in the Spirit. Or the contrast between living under the Old Covenant and living under the New Covenant.

You see, Jesus has invaded our lives. Further down in John 15, it says,

> You did not choose Me, but I chose you and appointed you that
> you should go and bear fruit, and that your fruit should remain,
> that whatever you ask the Father in My name He may give you.
> (John 15:16)

There's a lot of talk today about us choosing Jesus—about our choice to follow and respond to the gospel. In one sense, I understand that kind of language. But the reality is that Jesus chose you.

Jesus sought you out. He wanted to enter into a relationship with you. And He wants to take over, so you might become more and more like Him. If you really want to start growing and bearing much fruit, then you're going to let Jesus rearrange things in your life.

The life of a disciple of Jesus is a life rearranged. Jesus accepts you as you are. And He loves you as you are. But He doesn't let you stay

*The life of a disciple of Jesus is a life rearranged.*

that way. Your entire life is a process of Jesus conforming you into His image.

I was meditating on Romans 12:2. That verse speaks of not being conformed to this world. As the JB Phillips New Testament Translation puts it, "Don't allow the world to press you into its mold." I like that picture. Because whatever gets pressed into a mold becomes that form.

You've probably noticed that the world system we live in has a form. It has an ideal. Although it shifts and changes, the root of that form is godlessness. It's a world without God, without accountability. It's a world that's a lot like the book of Judges where everyone does what is right in their own eyes. There's a general emptiness in the world. And those who are separated from Jesus are spending their entire lives trying to fill that emptiness.

And the ones in the world with the most money and the greatest notoriety tend to be some of the most miserable. It seems that every day the news has another story about a celebrity who goes into rehab, checks in for mental health treatment, or even takes their own life. They're unable to cope.

Unfortunately, that's not just a worldly thing. Many believers have a hard time coping with the difficulties of life. When the challenges of life come, you have a choice. You can abide in Christ—the perfect place of peace. Or you can follow the way of the world and choose coping mechanisms that amount to idolatry. The worldly options will give you temporary peace. But those things will not give you any permanent, eternal help.

The solution to your problems is to abide—to live moment by moment in dependence on Jesus Christ. Moment . . . by . . . moment.

As Jesus taught His disciples to pray, He told them to ask God for their daily bread (Matthew 6:11). When was the last time that daily bread was of great concern to you? I know that even in a world of great excess, there are those who struggle. But generally, in our culture, I haven't met too many in the body of Christ who really struggle with daily bread.

Now, there are financial struggles. I'm not speaking about that. And I know some who have difficulties with paying the rent. Not too long ago, someone asked me for prayer because he needed $1,000 for his rent. His face showed great concern. He had an emergency, so he used the rent money for that.

So I laid hands on him, and we prayed together. And he left with peace and hope because we had sought the Lord. Well, wouldn't you know it? The day before his rent was due, the thousand bucks showed up. He got his tax refund. And it's a testimony to God.

Whether it's your daily bread or a mortgage payment, Jesus taught us that we need to live a life of dependence on Him, moment by moment. And if we can learn how to reduce our lives down to a moment-by-moment dependence on Jesus, we'll have peace from Him—moment by moment.

We need to obey God. He told us to cast our cares on Him because He cares for us (1 Peter 5:7). When you're relying on Jesus moment by moment, that's when you're abiding in Him.

The word abide in John 15:4 comes from the Greek word meno. And it simply means to remain; to dwell; to stay put.[1] It speaks of intimacy, closeness, and a permanent attachment.

I like how the Message paraphrase puts it. It says,

Live in me. Make your home in Me just as I do in you. In the same way that a branch can't bear grapes by itself but only by being joined to the vine, you can't bear fruit unless you are joined with Me. (John 15:4 (The Message))

I like that phrase, "Make your home in Me." That's a great picture.

When you're on your way home, you're not just trying to get close to your house. You don't go to the street you live on and walk into any house. No, you have a habit. And it's a good habit. You go to *your* home. You go to the place God gave you to dwell in. That place is your refuge. It's where you rest, sleep, eat, and enjoy family and friends. It's your home.

Just like you do with your physical home, make your spiritual home in Jesus. Make it in *Him*.

The New Living Translation says, "Yes, I am the Vine; you are the branches. Those who remain in Me, and I in them, will produce much fruit. For apart from Me you can do nothing" (John 15:5 (NLT)).

So, here's the key. The way to deal with your past—with the issues that inflame your emotions and the great hurt that you've endured from the consequences of your own bad decisions or someone else's—is to remain in Christ. Because the alternative is to run around, carelessly and aimlessly, like we used to.

We wandered aimlessly before we were saved. There was really no purpose or goal. We were living life in any way that we wanted. And if we defined something in a certain way and hit our own definition, we felt sort of good.

But we only find strength and fruit when we abide in Jesus—when we remain and stay put in His presence. So how do you do that? What happens when you abide in Jesus? It's not some esoteric, spiritual teaching where you sit on your couch without moving. But there's a way you can abide in Him.

## *An Attitude of Belief*

Abiding begins with a confession of faith. It's a confession that you trust Jesus and His sufficiency in your life. It's where you know the Word of God and begin to speak it forth into your life.

For example, do you have a care today? If you do, confess the Scripture that says to cast all your cares upon God because He cares for you (1 Peter 5:7). Tell yourself, *I'm going to cast my cares upon You today, God.* When you do, that's a statement of abiding. You say, *I'm not going to run to the bottle. I'm not going to get worked up by it. I'm not going to get mad about it. But I'm going to cast my care upon You today, God, because that's what You said to do.* And you can rehearse the whole thing before the Lord in your prayer time.

It begins with a confession, a statement of agreement with God's Word. Of course, God's Word is true whether you confess it—whether you agree with it—or not. It stands true. But to activate it in your life and enjoy what it says, you declare it. You say, *Lord, I'm going to cast this care upon You today.*

Then, abiding is followed with a steady obedience. Jesus said in John 14:15, "If you love Me, keep My commandments." Jesus said *if* you love Him. If Jesus came to you today and said, "I've got a quick question for you. Do you love Me?" What would you say? I hope you would answer, "Yes, of course."

And you know what Jesus would say? "Keep My commandments." And His commandments are not burdensome (1 John 5:3). His yolk is easy, and His burden is light (Matthew 11:30). Keep His commandments. That's the root of abiding—obedience.

Think about it. As you're saying, *Father, I come to You in prayer*, you're in a place of obedience. As you start speaking forth the Word of something that's ministering to you, you're in obedience. Your mind is focused. Your lips are following. And your actions will follow that. It starts with a confession. And it's followed up through obedience.

The *how* of abiding doesn't begin with a work. It's not a work that gets you there but an attitude. It's an attitude of believing what God has said.

You know, you already live with an attitude of belief in other things. When you're out somewhere and you're ready to go home, you go there and walk into your house. When you go home, you believe that's your home. You actually head in that direction.

You don't talk to Siri and say, "I forgot where I live. Can you just take me home?" No, you're confident. You know where you live. It's so common to you that you don't even speak out loud. You don't get in your car and tell yourself, *I'm going to go home. I live at 123 Main Street, and I'm going to get there in 15 minutes.* You don't do that. You have done it so many times that it's very natural for you. And your attitude—your belief—is that you're going to your home.

When it comes to your relationship with Jesus Christ, it's the same. When your mind is stirring and you can't control it—when your thoughts and feelings are overwhelming you—you could tell yourself, *I'm going to go home spiritually. I'm overwhelmed by my thoughts, Lord. And I'm coming home.*

It begins with an attitude of going home. And it's followed by an attitude of dependence on Jesus. That requires humility. You need to admit that you can't produce any fruit on your own.

Sometimes, it seems like you need to hurry because you've just got to gather your thoughts. But you're unable to gather your thoughts spiritually without the power of the Holy Spirit. It starts with Jesus. Jesus doesn't show up in the middle. It begins with Him. And even if you're able to gather your thoughts for a few moments, apart from Christ, those thoughts are going to come back bigger and harder. It's the reality of living in this world.

How does that relate to the past? The past is a great accuser —especially with the things we regret, the things we wish had never happened, and the situations we would avoid if we had another chance. Yet, who you are now is based on everything you did in your past.

As we learned, the Bible says there is therefore now no condemnation to those who are in Christ (Romans 8:1). What's another way of describing being in Christ? Abiding. You see, the Bible is one message. It's all about getting us to Jesus. Jesus took care of all our sin by taking our punishment on Himself. Because of what He did, we have a refuge in God.

When the Bible talks about God being our refuge, it speaks of abiding. In Proverbs 18:10, it says, "The name of the LORD is a strong tower; the righteous run to it and are safe." That's speaking of abiding.

We turn that around as if we actually have to run. You may think, *The name of the Lord is a strong tower. But the tower is way over there, and I have no energy to get way over there.* But it's a picture of trusting God. Just change your mind. It's not about you and your works. It's a mindset. And it starts with an attitude of belief.

## An Attitude of Dependence

You know yourself. And you know if you have an attitude of dependence—if you depend on God or if you depend on yourself. One of the greatest barriers to an attitude of dependence is pride. When you've failed, you can't be dependent on Him until you acknowledge your failure, receive God's forgiveness, and abide in Him again.

The person who is the most disappointed in your failures is you. We get so disappointed in ourselves. We kick ourselves. We replay the failure and tell ourselves, *I wish I'd never done that.*

There are things in my life now that are consequences of things I did years ago. And believe me, I wish I hadn't done them.

One of the things I teach the men and women who serve in our church is not to use email for difficult conversations. I use email less and less. A sentence or two in an email is all I'll do. And even then, I can mess up just a sentence or two.

I received a difficult email soon after the passing of my son. When I got it, I couldn't believe my eyes. I thought, *What is this? I can't believe this. I can't believe that they believe what they wrote about me and my family.*

So, what did I do? Did I take that email before the Lord like King Hezekiah did and ask, *God, what would you like me to do, my great defender with this email*? Did I set up an altar in my house? Or climb the little mountain in my office and seek the Lord like Moses did?

No. I sat down in my office, opened up my laptop, and began to answer that email—point by point. You know, it was a very difficult time. And tensions were very high.

My other son had just come back from Bible college. He walked by my office and said, "Dad, don't do that. Don't write the email. You know you're not supposed to use email like that. We should pray." And I told him, "No, no, that was for you. I'm the exception." Or some dumb thing like that. And I was serious.

And my wife was in the kitchen, saying, "Don't write that email!" And I'm like, "No."

After I wrote the email, I sent it to my wife and asked her to read it. I don't remember exactly how it all went. But nobody approved the sending of that email, including God.

Yet, I remember hitting the send button. And you can't take it back after that. I remember how self-justified I was. I anticipated how that email would vindicate my family and the situation. But it did none of those things. It only emboldened the enemy to stir up more strife and more difficulty. To this day, that email is part of some of the difficulties we face as a family. It's unbelievable.

You see, we all have things we regret. If I had the chance to go back, I would have never sent it. And I'm sharing it with you, so you don't commit the same failure that I did. Instead, take it to God like Hezekiah did (2 Kings 19:14–19). Lay it before the Lord and let Him take care of it.

As Pastor Chuck Smith taught us, you have two choices when it comes to defending yourself. The first one is to go ahead and defend yourself. You have the freedom to do that. And God will allow you to do so. But with what resources? An email? A few choice words? An argument? You'll be limited by your own resources.

Or you can choose the second option. By faith, you can let God defend you. In both the Old and the New Testaments, we see examples of those who abided in God and allowed Him to do the work. As you allow God to be your defense, you're depending on His righteousness. You choose to believe that His perfect justice will take care of you, as you did when you were first born again.

*We don't know everything. But God does.*

And then you can abide in Him by faith. Don't rely on your own crafty words or your own ideas. Even in our best-crafted strategies, we have limited knowledge. Have you noticed that? None of us has absolute knowledge. We don't know everything. But God does. When you let God defend you, you're no longer relying on your own works.

The fruit comes from abiding. It begins with an attitude of belief, a mindset. And then you follow it with an attitude of dependence and humility. As you do, remember three things.

First, believing is not so much a work as it is rest. Belief is actually resting on the promises of God. Resting in Him. Receiving. Patiently trusting Him.

Second, abiding involves an awareness of God's presence in our lives. Abiding is not a feeling. It's an acknowledgment that God is with you.

Finally, abiding involves surrender. When you abide in Jesus, you surrender your will to God's will. The alternative is placing yourself in the position of God. When you're not abiding in Him, you're doing things your own way. You're not trusting Him.

The habit of a moment-by-moment surrender to God is very fruitful. The fruit that God is looking for in our lives is not something we can produce ourselves.

### Abiding Is the Solution

The fruit of being free from your past is not something you can produce on your own. You can't do it in your own strength. You can't get free by running away as fast as you can from it. The solution is to abide.

Many of us get frustrated and upset because we're so active. We work hard. We measure today's success by comparing it with yesterday's. If we did more, we feel good about ourselves. If we did less, we feel bad. We offer our works to God to be well-pleasing to Him. For a time, it's okay. You're able to keep up. But the reality is that failure is just up ahead.

Then what do you do when you fail? You stumble. You were depending on your own works.

When you're not abiding, you depend on yourself. And you compare yourself with others to see how you're doing.

For example, if you go to a midweek service at your church, you will probably notice that there are fewer people there than in a weekend service. You may be tempted to feel like you're better than those who didn't come. You might even think to yourself, *Well, you know what? I made it here. Where are all the slackers? What are they doing tonight?* And before you know it, you're in a place of judgment. You're judging yourself better and others worse. That's not a place of abiding.

The place of abiding is when you think, *Man, it's so good to be in the house of the Lord. I want to be there as much as I can. And if I can't be there, I'll be somewhere else. But wherever I am, I'll be abiding in Jesus Christ. I'll be abiding in the presence of the Lord, and He in me.* Because "without Me," Jesus said, "you can do nothing."

Jesus also said,

> If anyone does not abide in Me, he is cast out as a branch and is withered; and they gather them and throw them into the fire, and they are burned. If you abide in Me, and My words abide in you, you will ask what you desire, and it shall be done for you. By this My Father is glorified, that you bear much fruit; so you will be My disciples.
>
> As the Father loved Me, I also have loved you; abide in My love. If you keep My commandments, you will abide in My love, just as I have kept My Father's commandments and abide in His love. (John 15:6–10)

Did you know that the moment you were born again, you started abiding in Christ? It's the closest thing I can think of to a time of pure abiding in Jesus.

When I was born again, I didn't know the Bible. I didn't know how to pray. I only knew that God loved me, He offered to forgive me of my sins through the finished work of Jesus Christ, and I needed to leave my sins. I had a very elementary view of God. I knew that God was God, and I was not. But I didn't know a lot. I didn't know where the books of the Bible were. We didn't even have a Bible in our house.

Yet, the finished work of Jesus Christ descended upon me at that moment in a very pure way. I didn't understand the word abide or know what the Greek word meno meant. But my pastor said, "From now on, you're going to enjoy Jesus Christ for the rest of your life. He lives in you, and you live in Him."

And my response? "That's awesome! This is crazy. God's in me, and I'm in Him?" I didn't walk out wondering, *What in the world does that mean?* Instead, I thought, *Man, this is an amazing life. I wonder what I need to learn. I wonder what's next?*

I was so dependent on God until I started reading the Bible. Then I got a little smart. I began to argue with God and disrupt my own life. Then I met the guys who came to the door, and they disrupted me. And then I got in trouble at work, and it disrupted me.

What happened? I had started with a simple, abiding relationship with Jesus Christ. My mindset began with thinking, *Jesus, You're so good to me. I'll do anything you say. Go anywhere you tell me. I'll live my life any way that you want. My life belongs to You.*

You see, if you abide in Jesus and His words—His teachings—abide in you, then you can ask for whatever you desire, and He'll give it to you (John 15:7). Jesus' words are life.

How many of us simply ask the Lord, "Please free me from my past." The key is to be abiding in Christ and to have His words abiding in you. How often? Moment by moment.

It's an abiding *life*, not an abiding *act.* It's not a one-time thing. You need to abide moment by moment. It's an abiding life, not

> *It's an abiding life, not an abiding act. It's not a one-time thing.*

a life filled with performance. It's a lifetime of abiding.

Fruit comes in our lives, not through work, but through relationship. God desires to work through us. God promises that if you are communing with Jesus, He will give you the desires of your heart. Your prayers will be answered.

That doesn't mean you can name something from God and claim it. You can't decide you're going to claim your riches or claim your healing. This verse has been twisted by some because they don't understand what Jesus is teaching here.

Jesus' teaching is very simple. As you abide in Christ moment by moment, His desires become your desires. Your prayers start to be in tune with Him. You begin asking for things that will glorify the Father. Your life reflects more and more of Jesus because you desire to do what pleases the Father.

It's the fruit of abiding when you see your prayers answered. When I prayed with that person about his rent, I wasn't sure what God was going to do. But the desire of my heart at that moment was to pray that he would be able to pay his rent—to take his problem to the Lord. God was the One who could solve it.

Religious legalism is in the Church today. It involves an air of criticism, nitpicking every point and dividing the Church.

I don't know if you've noticed, but we live in a culture where people don't know how to disagree with one another without trying to destroy the other person. It's okay to have disagreements, even in the body of Christ.

Like-mindedness in the body of Christ doesn't mean that we agree about every single thing. That's called conformity. And the Bible says that we're only to be conformed to the image of Christ, not to one another. We don't want to become exact copies of each another. We want to become like Jesus.

Being like-minded means that we generally agree with one another. And when we're like-minded, we can learn how to disagree in love.

The Bible doesn't say that the world will know we're Jesus' disciples by our criticisms and our hyper-judgmentalism. No, Jesus said, "By this all will know that you are My disciples, if you have love for one another" (John 13:35). In fact, the Bible warns us not to bite and devour one another (Galatians 5:15). Can you imagine? We need to abide in Him.

Listen to a description of the Pharisees from Jesus' day:

One distinctive feature of the Pharisees was their strong commitment to observing the law of God as it was interpreted and applied by the scribes. Although the priests had been responsible for teaching and interpreting the Law in Old Testament times, many people had lost all respect for the priests because of the corruption in the Jerusalem priesthood. They looked to the scribes instead to interpret the Law for them. Some scribes were priests; many were not. Still, they lived pious, disciplined lives; and they had been trained to become experts in the Law. It was natural, then, for people to follow their leading rather than that of the priests.[2]

The Pharisees were dedicated men of the Word. But the problem was that they missed the intent of the Bible. Instead of hitting their hearts, it went right to their heads. They were theologically right. But in love and practice, they were very wrong. And Jesus condemned them for it. Jesus didn't tell those who were caught up in sin, "Woe to you." He told the Pharisees, "Woe to you" (*see, e.g.*, Matthew 23:13).

Here's an example of how God's Word missed the Pharisees' hearts. The Pharisees were very precise in their tithing. If they had a little garden with little mint bushes, they would make sure they tithed based on any growth (Matthew 23:23). But when their parents needed help, they would take money from their parents (Matthew 15:3-9). They tithed their mint. But if their parents needed help, they would take that for themselves, financially. They were completely backward.

How did they miss it? They knew the Word, but the Word didn't abide in them. They were separated from Jesus Christ. But if they handled the Word properly, it would have brought them to Jesus Christ. That's the whole purpose of the law—to point out your needs so it will point you to Messiah.

So, the Pharisees could quote the Word to you. But the Word wasn't abiding in them. It wasn't in their hearts.

Remember how David wrote, "Your word I have hidden in my heart, that I might not sin against You" (Psalm 119:11). That's one of the advantages of memorizing Scripture. When you put God's Word in your heart, the Spirit of God can bring it back at the appropriate time and prevent you from sinning.

And Paul prayed that God "would grant you, according to the riches of His glory, to be strengthened with might through His Spirit in the inner man that Christ may dwell in your hearts through faith," and you would be rooted and grounded in love (Ephesians 3:16–17).

Eighteen inches can make all the difference. That 18 inches from your head to your heart—in your prayer life, in your evangelism, in your marriage, in your parenting, in your singleness, and in your abiding life. It's just 18 inches.

It's the difference between knowing something and experiencing it, between argumentation and heartbreak, and between contention and compassion. When you tend to argue, your heart's never touched by the needs around you. And then the needs around you are never touched by your heart.

The Church of Jesus Christ is on the earth to represent God. And God's heart is always broken by sin. A compassionate heart always desires to help.

What's the difference between the heart and the head? Well, the heart doesn't let go of things so easily. It's at the core of who you are. Both the Hebrews and the Greeks believed this. It's the sum of your love and adoration. The heart speaks of the totality of your person.

Along with love and adoration, bitterness and contempt can reside in your heart. And it sticks there. It's why the Bible warns us against letting a root of bitterness spring up in our lives (Hebrews 12:15).

But our minds? Our minds are not so permanent. While our hearts tend to hold on to things, our mind changes. We probably change our minds a thousand times a day. On a dime, we change lanes. Or we change our drinks at the coffee shop. Our minds are constantly changing.

If the Word of God isn't abiding in our hearts, we will quickly change our minds away from the truth. When we move away from the truth, we're no longer abiding in Christ. And, if you pay attention, you almost always change your mind to benefit yourself, not to glorify the Father.

Freedom from your past is an abiding life. Jesus said, "If anyone desires to come after Me, let him deny himself, and take up his cross, and follow Me" (Matthew 16:24). A life of abiding—of faith and dependence—brings great love and peace into your life. It results in a peace that surpasses all understanding.

As the Bible tells us,

> Be anxious for nothing, but in everything by prayer and supplication, with thanksgiving, let your requests be made known to God; and the peace of God, which surpasses all understanding, will guard your hearts and minds through Christ Jesus. (Philippians 4:6–7)

The abiding life is where it's at. Even as you're reading this book, you've been abiding. You've been staying put and receiving God's Word as unto the Lord.

Freedom from your past is found moment by moment, abiding in Christ. You know as well as I do that you can't unsend that email. You can't undo the past any more than you can unscramble an egg.

But you can live the life that God has given you at this moment. You can abide, trusting in Him. You can stay put, casting all your cares upon Him. You can search the Bible for passages that speak life to you—ones that relate to the sin issue in your life or to an issue that troubles you. You can find a list of Scriptures that talk about different issues in your life—like worry, anxiety, or fear at EdTaylor.org. The Bible has a lot to say about the things we deal with in our lives.

As you meditate on God's Word, confess it. Remain in Jesus. Trust Him. Enjoy your relationship with Him. Remember that God will do the work in your life as you abide in Him.

# CHAPTER SEVEN

## Dealing With Your Identity

Do you remember the true story about Rahab the harlot? Before the Israelites crossed over the Jordan River, Joshua sent two men to check out the land that God had promised to them. Rahab hid the men so they would be safe from the king of Jericho. She knew that God had given them the land (Joshua 2).

Based on her faith, God ensured that Rahab and her family were saved when He brought down the wall of Jericho and delivered the city into the Israelites' hands (Joshua 6:22–23, 25). God redeemed Rahab. He even gave her the privilege of being in the genealogy of Jesus (Matthew 1:5).

There are times when you're reading through a passage of Scripture and something leaps off the page. There was a time when I was reading through James and that happened. It said,

> Likewise, was not Rahab the harlot also justified by works when she received the messengers and sent them out another way? (James 2:25)

Three words jumped off of the page: *Rahab the harlot.* Now that's a horrible name to have. Wouldn't you agree? Rahab the harlot. Her first, middle, and last names. Rahab the harlot. Always remembered for her harlotry. And that's how she's known. Even here, James reminds us, this Rahab is the harlot that we met back in Joshua. Rahab the harlot. How sad.

But then you fast forward into heaven. And you think, *Will Rahab be known in heaven as Rahab the harlot?*

Think about it. We're all together. And you want to meet people. So you say, "Hey, where's Abraham?" "He's over there, that long line."

You don't want to wait in that line. So you ask, "Where's John the Baptist?" Then you notice that line's long too. Then you ask, "Where's Rahab the harlot?" And you hear, "Shhhhh!"

There is no Rahab the harlot in heaven. She's Rahab the saint. She's Rahab the redeemed—Rahab the washed and cleansed. She's Rahab the changed life. The one who loves Jesus. We won't identify people in heaven by their sin. We'll identify people by their Savior. So you won't be using those words in heaven.

Sometimes families can be like that, even if they're believers. They hold your past against you, even in the present. You may be known by your failures—as the black sheep of the family. They may say things like, "Oh, here comes you know who, the one who did you know what." You may even hold your failures against yourself, reminding yourself that you've always been the black sheep of the family.

I know we have our own feelings about people in our families. But may God convict us. Let us be compassionate with people in our families. Be patient with them. May the Lord help us not to identify people by their sin and by their failure, always holding the past up before them.

Rahab? Rahab's a saint. Rahab is no longer Rahab the harlot. Thomas isn't Thomas the doubter anymore. Peter isn't Peter the denier.

And you're not defined by your sin either. You're identified by your Savior. In the eyes of God, you're seen as perfect in Christ. You are a new creation in Jesus (2 Corinthians 5:17). In Christ, you're clean (John 15:3) and complete (Colossians 2:10). You're righteous and holy (Ephesians 4:24). You are no longer defined by your sin.

Jesus has freed you and given you life. Because you've received liberty from Him, your faith does not have to be dead, useless, or lifeless. Instead, let your life bring glory and honor to God. As Jesus told us, "Let your light so shine before men, that they may see your good works and glorify your Father in heaven" (Matthew 5:16).

As you abide in Jesus, day by day and moment by moment, spend time meditating on the promises God has given you about who you are in Christ. As we've learned, if you're a born-again believer, you're in Christ. Remind yourself daily about who you are in Him.

But remember—God's promises about who you are in Christ are secondary to the God who keeps His promises. God's promises are great and wonderful. And our faith is in *God's* ability to keep His promises, not in *our* ability to remember them. Our faith is in the God who gives power, not in our ability to submit to Him. Our faith is in the God who does the work, not in our ability to recognize His work.

Did you know that God does a lot in your life that you don't even recognize? Even though you don't see it, He still loves you. Aren't you glad you're not saved by seeing

> *Your faith should be in God—not in what He does and not in what He gives.*

everything that God does? God is doing things that He hasn't revealed to you yet. Your faith should be in God—not in what He does and not in what He gives. Your faith should be in *who* He is.

God's promises reveal His character and nature. That's where life is. Life is found in Jesus Christ. And it's conveyed to us from the inside out. Grace is amazing. A few minutes of Bible study doesn't even plumb the depths of the power of God in your life.

So, as you think about who you are in Christ, remember that your position in Christ is based on God's ability to keep you there. Your position in Christ is not based on your ability to remember who you are in Christ. Even when you forget who you are in Christ, God's promises remain true. Our God is faithful (2 Timothy 2:13).

Here's a list of 90 ways that you are in Christ. Take time to think about these truths. Don't rush through them. I challenge you to take a few months to go through the list. Each day, take a different truth and meditate on it. Soak it in. Ask God to help you believe the promises He's given you about your nature as a born-again believer.

In Christ:

## 1. You have been healed.

> But He was wounded for our transgressions, He was bruised for our iniquities; the chastisement for our peace was upon Him, and by His stripes we are healed. (Isaiah 53:5)

## 2. You are the salt of the earth.

> You are the salt of the earth; but if the salt loses its flavor, how shall it be seasoned? It is then good for nothing but to be thrown out and trampled underfoot by men. (Matthew 5:13)

## 3. You are the light of the world.

> You are the light of the world. A city that is set on a hill cannot be hidden. (Matthew 5:14)

## 4. You are commissioned to make disciples.

Go therefore and make disciples of all the nations, baptizing them in the name of the Father and of the Son and of the Holy Spirit, teaching them to observe all things that I have commanded you; and lo, I am with you always, even to the end of the age. (Matthew 28:19–20)

## 5. You are a child of God.

But as many as received Him, to them He gave the right to become children of God, to those who believe in His name. (John 1:12)

## 6. You have eternal life.

My sheep hear My voice, and I know them, and they follow Me. And I give them eternal life, and they shall never perish; neither shall anyone snatch them out of My hand. (John 10:27–28)

## 7. You have been given peace.

Peace I leave with you, My peace I give to you; not as the world gives do I give to you. Let not your heart be troubled, neither let it be afraid. (John 14:27)

## 8. You are part of the true vine, a channel of Christ's life.

I am the true vine, and My Father is the vinedresser.

   . . .

I am the vine, you are the branches. He who abides in Me,

and I in him, bears much fruit; for without Me you can do nothing. (John 15:1, 5)

## 9. You are clean.

You are already clean because of the word which I have spoken to you. (John 15:3)

## 10. You are Christ's friend.

No longer do I call you servants, for a servant does not know what his master is doing; but I have called you friends, for all things that I heard from My Father I have made known to you. (John 15:15)

## 11. You have been chosen and appointed by Christ to bear His fruit.

You did not choose Me, but I chose you and appointed you that you should go and bear fruit, and that your fruit should remain, that whatever you ask the Father in My name He may give you. (John 15:16)

## 12. You have been given glory.

And the glory which You gave Me I have given them, that they may be one just as We are one. (John 17:22)

## 13. You have been justified—completely forgiven and made righteous.

Therefore, having been justified by faith, we have peace with God through our Lord Jesus Christ. (Romans 5:1)

## 14. You died with Christ and to the power of sin's rule over your life.

What shall we say then? Shall we continue in sin that grace may abound? Certainly not! How shall we who died to sin live any longer in it? Or do you not know that as many of us as were baptized into Christ Jesus were baptized into His death? Therefore we were buried with Him through baptism into death, that just as Christ was raised from the dead by the glory of the Father, even so we also should walk in newness of life.

For if we have been united together in the likeness of His death, certainly we also shall be in the likeness of His resurrection, knowing this, that our old man was crucified with Him, that the body of sin might be done away with, that we should no longer be slaves of sin. (Romans 6:1–6)

## 15. You are a slave of righteousness.

And having been set free from sin, you became slaves of righteousness. (Romans 6:18)

## 16. You are free from sin and enslaved to God.

But now having been set free from sin, and having become slaves of God, you have your fruit to holiness, and the end, everlasting life. (Romans 6:22)

## 17. You are free from condemnation forever.

There is therefore now no condemnation to those who are in Christ Jesus, who do not walk according to the flesh, but according to the Spirit. (Romans 8:1)

## 18. You are a son or daughter of God; spiritually, God is your father.

For as many as are led by the Spirit of God, these are sons of God. For you did not receive the spirit of bondage again to fear, but you received the Spirit of adoption by whom we cry out, "Abba, Father." (Romans 8:14–15; *see also* Galatians 3:26, 4:6)

## 19. You are a joint heir with Christ, sharing His inheritance with Him.

[A]nd if children, then heirs—heirs of God and joint heirs with Christ, if indeed we suffer with Him, that we may also be glorified together. (Romans 8:17)

## 20. You are more than a conqueror through Christ who loves you.

Yet in all these things we are more than conquerors through Him who loved us. (Romans 8:37)

## 21. You have faith.

For I say, through the grace given to me, to everyone who is among you, not to think of himself more highly than he ought to think, but to think soberly, as God has dealt to each one a measure of faith. (Romans 12:3)

## 22. You have been sanctified and called to holiness.

To the church of God which is at Corinth, to those who are sanctified in Christ Jesus, called to be saints, with all who in every place call on the name of Jesus Christ our Lord, both theirs and ours. (1 Corinthians 1:2)

## 23. You have been given grace.

I thank my God always concerning you for the grace of God which was given to you by Christ Jesus. (1 Corinthians 1:4)

## 24. You have been placed into Christ by God.

But of Him you are in Christ Jesus, who became for us wisdom from God—and righteousness and sanctification and redemption. (1 Corinthians 1:30)

## 25. You have received God's Spirit so you might know the things that God has freely given you.

Now we have received, not the spirit of the world, but the Spirit who is from God, that we might know the things that have been freely given to us by God. (1 Corinthians 2:12)

## 26. You have been given the mind of Christ.

For "who has known the mind of the LORD that he may instruct Him?" But we have the mind of Christ. (1 Corinthians 2:16 (quoting Isaiah 40:13))

## 27. You are a temple—a dwelling place—of God, and His Spirit and life dwell in you.

Do you not know that you are the temple of God and that the Spirit of God dwells in you? (1 Corinthians 3:16; *see also* 1 Corinthians 6:19)

## 28. You are united to the Lord and are one spirit with Him.

But he who is joined to the Lord is one spirit with Him. (1 Corinthians 6:17)

## 29. You have been bought with a price; you are not your own; you belong to God.

Or do you not know that your body is the temple of the Holy Spirit who is in you, whom you have from God, and you are not your own? For you were bought at a price; therefore glorify God in your body and in your spirit, which are God's. (1 Corinthians 6:19–20; *see also* 1 Corinthians 7:23)

## 30. You are called.

But as God has distributed to each one, as the Lord has called each one, so let him walk. And so I ordain in all the churches. (1 Corinthians 7:17)

## 31. You are a member of Christ's body.

Now you are the body of Christ, and members individually. (1 Corinthians 12:27; *see also* Ephesians 5:30)

## 32. You are victorious through Jesus Christ.

But thanks be to God, who gives us the victory through our Lord Jesus Christ. (1 Corinthians 15:57)

## 33. You have been established, anointed, and sealed by God; God gave you the Holy Spirit as a pledge that guarantees your inheritance to come.

Now He who establishes us with you in Christ and has anointed us is God. (2 Corinthians 1:21; *see also* Ephesians 1:13–14)

## 34. You are led by God in a triumphal procession.

Now thanks be to God who always leads us in triumph in Christ, and through us diffuses the fragrance of His knowledge in every place. (2 Corinthians 2:14)

## 35. You are, to God, the fragrance of Christ among those who are being saved.

For we are to God the fragrance of Christ among those who are being saved and among those who are perishing. (2 Corinthians 2:15)

## 36. You are being changed into the likeness of Christ.

But we all, with unveiled face, beholding as in a mirror the glory of the Lord, are being transformed into the same image from glory to glory, just as by the Spirit of the Lord. (2 Corinthians 3:18)

## 37. You no longer live for yourself since you have died, but for Christ.

For the love of Christ compels us, because we judge thus: that if One died for all, then all died; and He died for all, that those who live should live no longer for themselves, but for Him who died for them and rose again. (2 Corinthians 5:14–15)

## 38. You are a new creation.

Therefore, if anyone is in Christ, he is a new creation; old things have passed away; behold, all things have become new. (2 Corinthians 5:17)

## 39. You are reconciled to God and a minister of reconciliation.

Now all things are of God, who has reconciled us to Himself through Jesus Christ, and has given us the ministry of reconciliation, that is, that God was in Christ reconciling the world to Himself, not imputing their trespasses to them, and has committed to us the word of reconciliation. (2 Corinthians 5:18–19)

## 40. You have been made righteous.

For He made Him who knew no sin to be sin for us, that we might become the righteousness of God in Him. (2 Corinthians 5:21)

## 41. You have been given strength in exchange for your weakness.

Therefore I take pleasure in infirmities, in reproaches, in needs, in persecutions, in distresses, for Christ's sake. For when I am weak, then I am strong. (2 Corinthians 12:10)

## 42. You have been crucified with Christ; it is no longer you who live but Christ who lives in you.

I have been crucified with Christ; it is no longer I who live, but Christ lives in me; and the life which I now live in the flesh I live by faith in the Son of God, who loved me and gave Himself for me. (Galatians 2:20)

### 43. You are a son or daughter of God and one in Christ.

For you are all sons of God through faith in Christ Jesus.

. . .

There is neither Jew nor Greek, there is neither slave nor free, there is neither male nor female; for you are all one in Christ Jesus. (Galatians 3:26, 28)

### 44. You are Abraham's seed and an heir of the promise.

And if you are Christ's, then you are Abraham's seed, and heirs according to the promise. (Galatians 3:29)

### 45. You are an heir of God since you are a son or daughter of God.

And because you are sons, God has sent forth the Spirit of His Son into your hearts, crying out, "Abba, Father!" Therefore you are no longer a slave but a son, and if a son, then an heir of God through Christ. (Galatians 4:6–7)

### 46. You are a saint.

Paul, an apostle of Jesus Christ by the will of God,

To the saints who are in Ephesus, and faithful in Christ Jesus. (Ephesians 1:1; *see also* 1 Corinthians 1:2; Philippians 1:1; Colossians 1:2)

## 47. You have been blessed with every spiritual blessing.

Blessed be the God and Father of our Lord Jesus Christ, who has blessed us with every spiritual blessing in the heavenly places in Christ. (Ephesians 1:3)

## 48. You were chosen before the foundation of the world to be holy; you are without blame before God.

[J]ust as He chose us in Him before the foundation of the world, that we should be holy and without blame before Him in love. (Ephesians 1:4)

## 49. You were predestined—determined by God—to be adopted as His child.

[H]aving predestined us to adoption as sons by Jesus Christ to Himself, according to the good pleasure of His will. (Ephesians 1:5)

## 50. You have been sealed with the Holy Spirit.

In Him you also trusted, after you heard the word of truth, the gospel of your salvation; in whom also, having believed, you were sealed with the Holy Spirit of promise. (Ephesians 1:13)

## 51. You have been redeemed and forgiven; you are a recipient of God's lavish grace.

But God, who is rich in mercy, because of His great love with which He loved us. (Ephesians 2:4)

## 52. You have been made alive together with Christ.

[E]ven when we were dead in trespasses, made us alive together with Christ (by grace you have been saved). (Ephesians 2:5)

## 53. You have been raised up and seated with Christ in heaven.

[A]nd raised us up together, and made us sit together in the heavenly places in Christ Jesus. (Ephesians 2:6)

## 54. You are God's workmanship—His handiwork—born anew in Christ to do His work.

For we are His workmanship, created in Christ Jesus for good works, which God prepared beforehand that we should walk in them. (Ephesians 2:10)

## 55. You have direct access to God through the Spirit.

For through Him we both have access by one Spirit to the Father. (Ephesians 2:18)

## 56. You are a fellow citizen with the rest of God's family.

Now, therefore, you are no longer strangers and foreigners, but fellow citizens with the saints and members of the household of God. (Ephesians 2:19)

## 57. You may approach God with boldness, freedom, and confidence.

[I]n whom we have boldness and access with confidence through faith in Him. (Ephesians 3:12)

## 58. You are righteous and holy.

[A]nd that you put on the new man which was created according to God, in true righteousness and holiness. (Ephesians 4:24)

## 59. You are a citizen of heaven and are seated in heaven right now.

For our citizenship is in heaven, from which we also eagerly wait for the Savior, the Lord Jesus Christ. (Philippians 3:20; *see also* Ephesians 2:6)

## 60. You are capable.

I can do all things through Christ who strengthens me. (Philippians 4:13)

## 61. You have been rescued from the domain of Satan's rule and transferred to the kingdom of Christ.

He has delivered us from the power of darkness and conveyed us into the kingdom of the Son of His love. (Colossians 1:13)

## 62. You have been redeemed and forgiven of all your sins; the debt you owed has been canceled.

[I]n whom we have redemption through His blood, the forgiveness of sins. (Colossians 1:14)

## 63. You are blameless and free from accusation.

[I]n the body of His flesh through death, to present you holy, and blameless, and above reproach in His sight. (Colossians 1:22)

## 64. You are indwelt by Christ Himself.

To them God willed to make known what are the riches of the glory of this mystery among the Gentiles: which is Christ in you, the hope of glory. (Colossians 1:27)

## 65. You are firmly rooted in Christ and are being built up by Him.

[R]ooted and built up in Him and established in the faith, as you have been taught, abounding in it with thanksgiving. (Colossians 2:7)

## 66. You have been made complete.

[A]nd you are complete in Him, who is the head of all principality and power. (Colossians 2:10)

## 67. You have been spiritually circumcised; your old, unregenerate nature has been removed.

In Him you were also circumcised with the circumcision made without hands, by putting off the body of the sins of the flesh, by the circumcision of Christ. (Colossians 2:11)

## 68. You have been buried, raised, and made alive with Christ.

[B]uried with Him in baptism, in which you also were raised with Him through faith in the working of God, who raised Him from the dead. And you, being dead in your trespasses and the uncircumcision of your flesh, He has made alive together with Him, having forgiven you all trespasses. (Colossians 2:12–13)

## 69. You died with Christ and have been raised up with Him; your life is now hidden with Christ in God; Christ is now your life.

If then you were raised with Christ, seek those things which are above, where Christ is, sitting at the right hand of God. Set your mind on things above, not on things on the earth. For you died, and your life is hidden with Christ in God. When Christ who is our life appears, then you also will appear with Him in glory. (Colossians 3:1–4)

## 70. You are an expression of Christ's life because He is your life.

When Christ who is our life appears, then you also will appear with Him in glory. (Colossians 3:4)

## 71. You are chosen by God, holy, and dearly loved.

Therefore, as the elect of God, holy and beloved, put on tender mercies, kindness, humility, meekness, longsuffering. (Colossians 3:12)

## 72. You are a son or daughter of light and not of darkness.

You are all sons of light and sons of the day. We are not of the night nor of darkness. (1 Thessalonians 5:5)

## 73. You have been given a spirit of power, love, and self-discipline.

For God has not given us a spirit of fear, but of power and of love and of a sound mind. (2 Timothy 1:7)

## 74. You have been saved and set apart by God.

[W]ho has saved us and called us with a holy calling, not according to our works, but according to His own purpose and grace which was given to us in Christ Jesus before time began. (2 Timothy 1:9; *see also* Titus 3:5)

## 75. Jesus is not ashamed to call you his brother or sister because you are sanctified and one with the Sanctifier.

For both He who sanctifies and those who are being sanctified are all of one, for which reason He is not ashamed to call them brethren. (Hebrews 2:11)

## 76. You are a holy partaker of a heavenly calling.

Therefore, holy brethren, partakers of the heavenly calling, consider the Apostle and High Priest of our confession, Christ Jesus. (Hebrews 3:1)

## 77. You have the right to come boldly before God's throne to find mercy and grace in a time of need.

Let us therefore come boldly to the throne of grace, that we may obtain mercy and find grace to help in time of need. (Hebrews 4:16)

## 78. You have been born again.

[H]aving been born again, not of corruptible seed but incorruptible, through the word of God which lives and abides forever. (1 Peter 1:23)

## 79. You are one of God's living stones, being built up in Christ as a spiritual house.

[Y]ou also, as living stones, are being built up a spiritual house, a holy priesthood, to offer up spiritual sacrifices acceptable to God through Jesus Christ. (1 Peter 2:5)

Free from Your Past

## 80. You are a member of a chosen race, a royal priesthood, a holy nation, and a people for God's own possession.

> But you are a chosen generation, a royal priesthood, a holy nation, His own special people, that you may proclaim the praises of Him who called you out of darkness into His marvelous light; who once were not a people but are now the people of God, who had not obtained mercy but now have obtained mercy. (1 Peter 2:9–10)

## 81. You are an alien and stranger of this world in which you temporarily live.

> Beloved, I beg you as sojourners and pilgrims, abstain from fleshly lusts which war against the soul. (1 Peter 2:11)

## 82. You are an enemy of the devil.

> Beloved, I beg you as sojourners and pilgrims, abstain from fleshly lusts which war against the soul. (1 Peter 2:11)

## 83. You have been given exceedingly great and precious promises by God, by which you are a partaker of God's divine nature.

> [B]y which have been given to us exceedingly great and precious promises, that through these you may be partakers of the divine nature, having escaped the corruption that is in the world through lust. (2 Peter 1:4)

144

## 84. You are forgiven on account of Jesus' name.

I write to you, little children, because your sins are forgiven you for His name's sake. (1 John 2:12)

## 85. You are anointed by God.

But the anointing which you have received from Him abides in you, and you do not need that anyone teach you; but as the same anointing teaches you concerning all things, and is true, and is not a lie, and just as it has taught you, you will abide in Him. (1 John 2:27)

## 86. You are a child of God, and you will resemble Christ when He returns.

Behold what manner of love the Father has bestowed on us, that we should be called children of God! Therefore the world does not know us, because it did not know Him. Beloved, now we are children of God; and it has not yet been revealed what we shall be, but we know that when He is revealed, we shall be like Him, for we shall see Him as He is. (1 John 3:1–2)

## 87. You are loved.

In this is love, not that we loved God, but that He loved us and sent His Son to be the propitiation for our sins. (1 John 4:10)

## 88. You have life.

He who has the Son has life; he who does not have the Son of God does not have life. (1 John 5:12)

## 89. You are born of God, and the evil one—the devil— cannot touch you.

We know that whoever is born of God does not sin; but he who has been born of God keeps himself, and the wicked one does not touch him. (1 John 5:18)

## 90. You have been redeemed.

And they sang a new song, saying:

"You are worthy to take the scroll, and to open its seals; for You were slain, and have redeemed us to God by Your blood out of every tribe and tongue and people and nation, and have made us kings and priests to our God; and we shall reign on the earth." (Revelation 5:9)

# Afterword

Friend, I know dealing with your past will include more than just reading this book. It's not as simple as some people think. However, it is probably simpler than you've felt before. God is ready to work on your behalf right now!

I know that God will use this book, and the things you've learned, to release you from those things that hold you in bondage. As you choose to put the principles into practice, you will begin to experience the life you've always wanted to live.

It won't be easy. There will be setbacks. Keep making those forward-facing decisions that God will honor with the power and presence of His Holy Spirit.

If you need prayer, you can email me directly at ed@edtaylor.org or text me at 720-608-0012.

May the Lord bless you and strengthen you for the battle!

For this reason I bow my knees to the Father of our Lord Jesus Christ, from whom the whole family in heaven and earth is named, that He would grant you, according to the riches of His glory, to be strengthened with might through His Spirit in the inner man, that Christ may dwell in your hearts through faith; that you, being rooted and grounded in love, may be able to comprehend with all the saints what is the width and length and depth and height—to know the love of Christ which passes knowledge; that you may be filled with all the fullness of God.

Now to Him who is able to do exceedingly abundantly above all that we ask or think, according to the power that works in us, to Him be glory in the church by Christ Jesus to all generations, forever and ever. Amen. (Ephesians 3:14–21)

# Notes

## 1. Dealing with Condemnation

1. *Merriam-Webster*, s.v. "condemn (*v.*)," accessed January 27, 2023, https://www.merriam-webster.com/dictionary/condemn.

## 2. Dealing with the Law of God

1. Olive Tree Bible Software, ed., *Olive Tree Enhanced Strong's Dictionary* (n.p.: Olive Tree, 2011), Strong's number h3724 ("price of a life, ransom").
2. Olive Tree, *Enhanced Strong's Dictionary*, h3722.

## 3. Dealing with Your Past

1. Olive Tree, *Enhanced Strong's Dictionary*, g1377.
2. Olive Tree, *Enhanced Strong's Dictionary*, h7368

## 4. Dealing with Forgiveness

1. This story is based on Ernest Hemingway's short story, *The Capital of the World*. Ernest Hemingway, "The Capital of the World," in *The First Forty-Nine Stories* (London: Jonathan Cape, 1946), 44.
2. These insights on forgiveness were developed from Craig Caster's pamphlet on forgiveness. *See* Craig Caster, *Forgiveness and Reconciliation Workbook* (El Cajon, CA: Family Discipleship Ministries, 2013).
3. Olive Tree, *Enhanced Strong's Dictionary*, g2675.

## 5. Dealing with Your Anger

1. Theopedia, s.v. "Anger," accessed February 2, 2023, https://www.theopedia.com/anger.
2. Mayumi Okuda et al., "Prevalence and Correlates of Anger in the Community: Results from a National Survey," National Center for Biotechnology Information (April 1, 2016), https://www.ncbi.nlm.nih.gov/pmc/ articles/PMC4384185/.
3. Mayo Clinic Staff, "Anger Management: 10 tips to tame your temper," *Mayo*

# Notes

*Clinic*, accessed January 28, 2023, https://www.mayoclinic.org/healthy-lifestyle/adult-health/in-depth/anger-management/art-20045434.

4. "AngerShotgun," Bible.org, accessed January 28, 2023, https://bible.org/illustration/anger-shotgun.

## 6. Dealing with the Present

1. Olive Tree, *Enhanced Strong's Dictionary*, g3306.
2. Ronald F. Youngblood, ed., *Nelson's New Illustrated Bible Dictionary* (Nashville, TN: Thomas Nelson, Inc., 1995), s.v. "Pharisees" (internal citations omitted).

# About the Author

Ed Taylor is the pastor of Calvary Church in Aurora, Colorado, which he, along with his family, has the privilege of serving and loving.

Growing up in Southern California, living a life of rebellious sin, Ed was born again through the ministry of Calvary Chapel Downey and was discipled there for eight years. In 1999, sensing the call of God, Ed and his family moved to the Denver area, hoping to be used by God in seeing a new church planted. In December of 1999, Calvary Church (Aurora, Colorado) began Sunday services and today continues to impact the community in dynamically glorious ways.

Pastor Ed's heart is to be transparent from the pulpit as he deeply desires everyone from all walks of life to embrace Jesus and grow in His grace.

Ed and his wife Marie have been married since 1989 and have three children, of which their eldest son Eddie went to be with the Lord in 2013. Ed and Marie also have a precious grandson, Eddie's son, Levi.

Ed is an author and blogger on EdTaylor.org, writing on life, ministry, and grief.

His Bible teaching ministry can be heard throughout the country through the "Abounding Grace" Radio Broadcast (heard locally on Grace FM Colorado) or through his podcast on leadership called Lead2Serve.

facebook.com/pastoredtaylor

twitter.com/calvarychurchco

instagram.com/pastoredtaylor

# Other Books by Ed Taylor

## Available at calvaryco.store and amazon.com

### God's Help for the Troubled Heart

Based on his own journey of healing, Pastor Ed Taylor will lead you through a series of Biblical reminders about God's faithfulness during times of suffering and pain. Also available in Spanish.

### Sure & Steady: *Learning and Growing in Pastoral Ministry*

Whether you're a pastor or a spiritual leader in your church, this workbook will guide you through the details and importance of pastoring and serving others. Also available in Spanish.

### Ordinary Servant: *Lessons In Loving Jesus and Serving His People*

Do you want to be someone that God can use to make a difference in this world? Examine the ministry of servanthood and learn how you can serve others with the heart of Jesus.

## Face Your Fears: *Learning to Trust God in Scary Times*

Are your fears holding you back from God's best in your life? If you're stuck and need deliverance, this book will provide Scriptural truth and encouragement to help you move from fear into faith. Also available in Spanish.

## You Will Make It Through

Find yourself refocused and encouraged as you look to Jesus to bring you through the hard and unpredictable trials in life.